Spelling Wisdom
Book Three
(American Version)

Learn today's 6,000 most frequently used words,
presented in the writings of great men and women of history

Compiled and Edited
by
Sonya Shafer

Spelling Wisdom, Book Three (American Version)
© 2006, Sonya Shafer

Published and printed by
Simply Charlotte Mason, LLC
P.O. Box 892
Grayson, Georgia 30017-0892

ISBN 978-1-61634-028-5

www.SimplyCharlotteMason.com

Contents
Spelling Wisdom, Book Three

Contents (cont.)
Spelling Wisdom, Book Three

Contents (cont.)
Spelling Wisdom, Book Three

Contents (cont.)
Spelling Wisdom, Book Three

Contents (cont.)
Spelling Wisdom, Book Three

Contents (cont.)
Spelling Wisdom, Book Three

www.SimplyCharlotteMason.com

Contents (cont.)
Spelling Wisdom, Book Three

Contents (cont.)
Spelling Wisdom, Book Three

Contents (cont.)
Spelling Wisdom, Book Three

Contents (cont.)
Spelling Wisdom, Book Three

Contents (cont.)
Spelling Wisdom, Book Three

Introduction

A Word about Dictation

Just as Charlotte Mason taught handwriting in the context of an interesting passage or text, so she taught spelling, not in isolated lists of words but in the context of useful and beautiful language.

We can present the child with a list of words to learn, such as: "am, will, can, I, ought." How much more pleasant to rearrange that list of words into an inspiring or interesting thought, like Charlotte Mason's motto for students: "I am, I can, I ought, I will."

Charlotte used this principle with prepared dictation to teach spelling, beginning in about the third or fourth grade. In prepared dictation, the student is given a passage to study before he is required to write it—the chief objective being to write it correctly.

Miss Mason believed that "the gift of spelling depends upon the power the eye possesses to 'take' (in a photographic sense) a detailed picture of a word; and this is a power and habit which must be cultivated in children from the first. When they have read 'cat,' they must be encouraged to see the word with their eyes shut, and the same habit will enable them to image 'Thermopylae.'"

She discouraged teachers from allowing their students to see a word incorrectly spelled, for "once the eye sees a misspelt word, that image remains; and if there is also the image of the word rightly spelt, we are perplexed as to which is which."

Of course, students will not spell every word correctly every time, therefore, it becomes "the teacher's business to prevent false spelling, and, if an error has been made, to hide it away, as it were, so that the impression may not become fixed."

"Dictation lessons, conducted in some such way as the following, usually result in good spelling."

(Quotations from *Home Education*, pp. 240, 241)

How to Use
Spelling Wisdom

1. Once or twice a week **give** your student a dictation exercise you want him to learn. Simply print or copy the exercise from this book. (You have permission to duplicate the exercises for use within your immediate household.)

2. Look through the exercise together and **identify** the words that you or the student thinks needs his attention in order to spell them confidently.

3. Instruct the student to **study** the identified words—one at a time—until he is sure he can spell every word in the exercise. This study period may take anywhere from a few minutes to several days, depending on the length of the exercise and the needs of the student. Set aside a little time each day for brief but consistent study of the exercise as needed. (See below for how to study a word.)

4. When the student is confident that he can spell every word in the exercise, **dictate** the passage to him one phrase at a time, saying the phrase only once. Pause after each phrase is spoken to allow him time to write it. Keep a careful eye on his efforts. If a word is misspelled, quickly cover it with a small self-stick note so its false spelling won't be engraved in the student's mind.

5. After the dictation is complete, the student should study any words that he misspelled and, when he is ready, **write** the words correctly on the self-stick notes.

How to Study a Word

You may want to work with younger or uncertain students to teach them how to study an unfamiliar word, as outlined below. Older students or students more accustomed to using the method below may study independently.

- Copy the word carefully, making sure it is spelled correctly.
- Look at the word until you can close your eyes and see it spelled correctly in your mind.
- Practice writing the word only if the teacher is nearby to immediately erase any misspellings.

Along with Charlotte's method of visualizing the word, we might add one or two study techniques for students who like to use their other senses in the learning process.
- Say the letters aloud in order while looking at the word.
- "Write" the word with your first finger on a sheet of paper or other smooth surface, being careful to look at the word and spell it correctly.

About *Spelling Wisdom*

When I read about Charlotte Mason's method of using prepared dictation to teach spelling, I loved the idea and wanted to use it. But I was concerned about missing some necessary words as I selected dictation passages to use. I felt very secure using my traditional spelling lists that I knew included the most frequently used words in the English language, which my children definitely needed to learn to spell.

So I decided to try to combine the two: dictation exercises that I could be sure included the most frequently used words in the English language. The *Spelling Wisdom* series is the result of that effort.

The five books' exercises become progressively longer and contain more difficult words as you work through the series. Each book contains 140 exercises. If you cover two exercises per week, you should be able to finish a *Spelling Wisdom* book in a little less than two school years. Charlotte began dictation exercises with students around the third or fourth grade. With that schedule in mind, here is a rough model of which books correspond to which grades:

Grades 3–5	Book One
Grades 5–7	Book Two
Grades 7–9	Book Three
Grades 9–11	Book Four
Grades 11, 12	Book Five

Content

The exercises cover a broad range of subjects and topics to reinforce Charlotte's love of a full and generous education. Because the books are not thematic, you can use and benefit from the exercises no matter what you may be studying in other school subjects.

I wanted to keep Miss Mason's high standards for beautiful thoughts and engaging narratives, so the sources of these exercises are speeches, letters, and quotations of famous people; excerpts from historical documents; descriptions of historical people and events; poetry; Scripture; excerpts from great literature; and selections from old readers and books for young people. Most of the passages were written prior to 1900. (I did find it necessary to write a few original exercises that involved the more modern words, like "infrastructure" and "computer.") Each book's bibliography and table of contents will provide more specific information as to which sources were used.

The 6,000 most-frequently-used English words included in these exercises are taken from A General Service List of English Words by Michael West (Longman, London 1953) and The Academic Word List by Coxhead (1998, 2000). We have also included more than 6,500 other words that we think well-educated children should know. These bonus words are in addition to those on the lists, making a total of more than 12,500 English words covered in the *Spelling Wisdom* series of books.

About Spelling Wisdom (cont.)

Index

The index in the back of each *Spelling Wisdom* book will give you a list of all the words included in that book's exercises. If you want to concentrate on or review a particular word, just look in the book's index to find any other exercises that use it. The index should also prove to be a friendly help if you spot a word or two in the child's written narrations that need some attention. You can easily find and assign a dictation exercise that uses the word in question and reinforces its correct spelling.

Spelling Variations

You may have noticed that the older writings contain some different spellings than we use today. For example, in Charlotte Mason's *Home Education* passage quoted at the beginning of this introduction, the word we spell today as "misspelled" was originally spelled "misspelt." Because the main objective of dictation is correct spelling, I updated such older words to modern spelling.

Two versions of the *Spelling Wisdom* series are available: American and British. The British version contains the British spelling preferences that I'm aware of. If I overlooked a possible alternate spelling, you can easily write your preferred spelling on the printed sheet that you give your student. (Then would you please e-mail me with the details of the change, or any other corrections, so I can change it in the book? Just send an e-mail to sonya@simplycharlottemason.com. Thank you!)

Poetry Variations

Many poets "take liberties" with word spellings in order to make the words fit in their assigned poetical places. Several of the poetry selections in these dictation exercises contained contracted words, such as "o'er" instead of "over." Since the goal of dictation is correct spelling, and missing letters don't help us reach that goal, I replaced contracted words with their spelled-out versions. You can easily enjoy the original form of the poems in your regular poetry studies, but for dictation purposes I thought the prudent path was to display the words correctly spelled.

Punctuation Variations

Because Charlotte advocated dictating "with a view to the pointing [punctuation], which the children are expected to put in as they write," I have attempted to edit the punctuation of the older passages to bring them more closely into conformity with modern punctuation guidelines. Encourage the children to make sure they are familiar with where the capital letters and punctuation marks go in their assigned exercises, even as they make sure they can spell all the words.

It is my hope that this collection of dictation exercises will make your journey more enjoyable and your path a little smoother on the "royal road to spelling."

(Quotations from *Home Education*, pp. 241, 242)

Exercise 1
Little Hammers
By Charlotte Mason

The habits of the child are, as it were, so many little hammers beating out by slow degrees the character of the man.

Exercise 2
Not To Excite Suspicion
From *Mansfield Park* by Jane Austen

Not to excite suspicion by her look or manner was now an object worth attaining.

Exercise 3
True Happiness
By Helen Keller

Many persons have a wrong idea of what constitutes true happiness. It is not attained through self-gratification but through fidelity to a worthy purpose.

Exercise 4
The Face of a Man
From *Wreck of the Golden Mary* by Charles Dickens

I admire machinery as much as any man and am as thankful to it as any man can be for what it does for us. But it will never be a substitute for the face of a man, with his soul in it, encouraging another man to be brave and true.

Exercise 5
Gone Fishing
From *The Pioneers* by James Fenimore Cooper

The old men received Oliver with welcoming nods, but neither drew his line from the water nor in the least varied his occupation. When Edwards had secured his own boat, he baited his hook and threw it into the lake without speaking.

Exercise 6
Dishonesty
From *Hunted Down* by Charles Dickens

I have known a vast quantity of nonsense talked about bad men not looking you in the face. Don't trust that conventional idea. Dishonesty will stare honesty out of countenance any day in the week if there is anything to be got by it.

Contagious Laughter
From *A Christmas Carol* by Charles Dickens

It is a fair, even-handed, noble adjustment of things that while there is infection in disease and sorrow, there is nothing in the world so irresistibly contagious as laughter and good humor.

Dreams
From *Nicholas Nickleby* by Charles Dickens

Dreams are the bright creatures of poem and legend, who sport on earth in the night season and melt away in the first beam of the sun, which lights grim care and stern reality on their daily pilgrimage through the world.

Let us hear the conclusion of the whole matter: Fear God and keep his commandments, for this is the whole duty of man. For God shall bring every work into judgment with every secret thing, whether it be good or whether it be evil.

Exercise 10
They Are Both Men
From *The Deerslayer* by James Fenimore Cooper

"But I do say they are both men—men of different races and colors and having different gifts and traditions, but in the main, with the same nature. Both have souls; and both will be held accountable for their deeds in this life."

A Swarm of Bees Worth Hiving
From *The Life of Jesus Christ for the Young* by Richard Newton

Be patient, Be prayerful, Be humble, Be mild,
Be wise as a Solon, Be meek as a child.

Be studious, Be thoughtful, Be loving, Be kind,
Be sure you make matter subservient to mind.

Be cautious, Be prudent, Be trustful, Be true,
Be courteous to all men, Be friendly with few.

Be temperate in argument, pleasure, and wine,
Be careful of conduct, of money, of time.

Be cheerful, Be grateful, Be hopeful, Be firm,
Be peaceful, benevolent, willing to learn;

Be courageous, Be gentle, Be liberal, Be just,
Be aspiring, Be humble, because you are dust.

Be penitent, circumspect, sound in the faith,
Be active, devoted; Be faithful to death.

Be honest, Be holy, transparent, and pure;
Be dependent, Be Christlike, and you'll be secure.

A Great Charm
From *Emma* by Jane Austen

Poverty certainly has not contracted her mind. I really believe if she had only a shilling in the world, she would be very likely to give away sixpence of it; and nobody is afraid of her—that is a great charm.

Exercise 13
Scrooge
From *A Christmas Carol* by Charles Dickens

External heat and cold had little influence on Scrooge. No warmth could warm, no wintry weather chill him. No wind that blew was bitterer than he, no falling snow was more intent upon its purpose, no pelting rain less open to entreaty.

Make Progress
By Sir Winston Churchill

Every day you may make progress. Every step may be fruitful. Yet there will stretch out before you an ever-lengthening, ever-ascending, ever-improving path. You know you will never get to the end of the journey. But this, so far from discouraging, only adds to the joy and glory of the climb.

Exercise 15
A Sprinkling of Powder
From *Nicholas Nickleby* by Charles Dickens

He wore a sprinkling of powder upon his head, as if to make himself look benevolent; but if that were his purpose, he would perhaps have done better to powder his countenance also, for there was something in its very wrinkles and in his cold restless eye which seemed to tell of cunning that would announce itself in spite of him.

The Society of Authors
From George Muller of Bristol by A.T. Pierson

There is open to us a society of people of the very first rank who will meet us and converse with us so long as we like, whatever our ignorance, poverty, or low estate—namely, the society of authors; and the key that unlocks their private audience-chamber is their books.

Sailing Over Angry Waters
From *The Pickwick Papers* by Charles Dickens

He was sailing over a boundless expanse of sea with a blood-red sky above and the angry waters lashed into fury beneath, boiling and eddying up on every side. There was another vessel before them, toiling and laboring in the howling storm, her canvas fluttering in ribbons from the mast.

The Best Actor
From *Mansfield Park* by Jane Austen

As far as she could judge, Mr. Crawford was considerably the best actor of all; he had more confidence than Edmund, more judgment than Tom, more talent and taste than Mr. Yates. She did not like him as a man, but she must admit him to be the best actor, and on this point there were not many who differed from her.

Grow in Christlikeness
From *George Muller of Bristol* by A.T. Pierson

He who lets no mercy of God escape thankful recognition, who never hesitates at once to abandon an evil or questionable practice, and who, instead of extenuating a sin because it is comparatively small, promptly confesses and forsakes it—such a man will surely grow in Christlikeness.

Loyal Sympathy
From *The Pickwick Papers* by Charles Dickens

A silent look of affection and regard when all other eyes are turned coldly away— the consciousness that we possess the sympathy and affection of one being when all others have deserted us—is a hold, a stay, a comfort in the deepest affliction, which no wealth could purchase or power bestow.

Exercise 21
At the Abbey
From *Emma* by Jane Austen

It was so long since Emma had been at the Abbey that as soon as she was satisfied of her father's comfort, she was glad to leave him and look around her—eager to refresh and correct her memory with more particular observation, more exact understanding of a house and grounds which must ever be so interesting to her and all her family.

My Little Book
From *The Pilgrim's Progress* by John Bunyan

If that a pearl may in a toad's head dwell,
And may be found too in an oyster-shell;
If things that promise nothing do contain
What better is than gold; who will disdain,
That have an inkling of it, there to look,
That they may find it? Now, my little book,
(Though void of all these paintings that may make
It with this or the other man to take)
Is not without those things that do excel
What do in brave but empty notions dwell.

Exercise 23
Jean Louis Ernest Meissonier
From *Pictures Every Child Should Know* by Mary Schell Hoke Bacon

Until this artist's time, people had been used only to great canvases and had grown to look for fine work only in much space, but here was an artist who could paint exquisitely a whole interior on a space said to be no "larger than his thumbnail." His work was called "microscopic," which meant that he gave great attention to details, painting very slowly.

Exercise 24
A Mere Unit
From *Nicholas Nickleby* by Charles Dickens

Although a man may lose a sense of his own importance when he is a mere unit among a busy throng, all utterly regardless of him, it by no means follows that he can dispossess himself, with equal facility, of a very strong sense of the importance and magnitude of his cares.

Exercise 25
The Letter
From *Mansfield Park* by Jane Austen

There was great food for meditation in this letter, and chiefly for unpleasant meditation; and yet, with all the uneasiness it supplied, it connected her with the absent, it told her of people and things about whom she had never felt so much curiosity as now, and she would have been glad to have been sure of such a letter every week.

Storms of Adversity
From *Sanders' Union Fourth Reader* by Charles W. Sanders

A smooth sea never made a skillful mariner. Neither do uninterrupted prosperity and success qualify man for usefulness or happiness. The storms of adversity, like the storms of the ocean, rouse the faculties and excite the invention, prudence, skill, and fortitude of the voyager.

Injustice
From *Great Expectations* by Charles Dickens

In the little world in which children have their existence—whosoever brings them up—there is nothing so finely perceived and so finely felt as injustice. It may be only small injustice that the child can be exposed to, but the child is small and its world is small and its rocking horse stands as many hands high.

Threatened with My Presence
From *Letters of Franz Liszt* by Franz Liszt

Dear Count,

Shall you like to have me again at Pest this year? I know not. In any case you are threatened with my presence from the 18th to the 22nd of next December. I shall come to you a little older, a little more matured, and, permit me to say, more finished an artist than I was when you saw me last year, for since that time I have worked enormously in Italy. I hope you have kept me in remembrance and that I may always count on your friendship, which is dear to me.

Towards the House
From *The Battle of Life* by Charles Dickens

There was a frosty rime upon the trees, which in the faint light of the clouded moon, hung upon the smaller branches like dead garlands. Withered leaves crackled and snapped beneath his feet as he crept softly on towards the house. The desolation of a winter night sat brooding on the earth and in the sky. But the red light came cheerily towards him from the windows; figures passed and re-passed there; and the hum and murmur of voices greeted his ear sweetly.

The Man of Business
From *The Pickwick Papers* by Charles Dickens

Mr. Pickwick took a seat and the paper, but instead of reading the latter, peeped over the top of it and took a survey of the man of business, who was an elderly, pimply-faced, vegetable-diet sort of man in a black coat, dark mixture trousers, and small black gaiters—a kind of being who seemed to be an essential part of the desk at which he was writing and to have as much thought or sentiment.

Sunshine

From *Mansfield Park* by Jane Austen

The sun was yet an hour and half above the horizon. She felt that she had, indeed, been three months there; and the sun's rays, falling strongly into the parlor, instead of cheering, made her still more melancholy, for sunshine appeared to her a totally different thing in a town and in the country. Here, its power was only a glare—a stifling, sickly glare, serving but to bring forward stains and dirt that might otherwise have slept.

How Do I Love Thee?
By Elizabeth Barrett Browning

How do I love thee? Let me count the ways.
I love thee to the depth and breadth and height
My soul can reach, when feeling out of sight
For the ends of Being and ideal Grace.
I love thee to the level of every day's
Most quiet need, by sun and candlelight.
I love thee freely, as men strive for Right;
I love thee purely, as they turn from Praise.
I love with a passion put to use
In my old griefs, and with my childhood's faith.
I love thee with a love I seemed to lose
With my lost saints, I love thee with the breath,
Smiles, tears, of all my life! and, if God choose,
I shall but love thee better after death.

Writing a Letter
From *The Pickwick Papers* by Charles Dickens

To ladies and gentlemen who are not in the habit of devoting themselves practically to the science of penmanship, writing a letter is no very easy task; it being always considered necessary in such cases for the writer to recline his head on his left arm, so as to place his eyes as nearly as possible on a level with the paper, while glancing sideways at the letters he is constructing, to form with his tongue imaginary characters to correspond. These motions, although unquestionably of the greatest assistance to original composition, retard in some degree the progress of the writer.

Midnight

From *Master Humphrey's Clock* by Charles Dickens

My old companion tells me it is midnight. The fire glows brightly, crackling with a sharp and cheerful sound, as if it loved to burn. The merry cricket on the hearth (my constant visitor), this ruddy blaze, my clock, and I seem to share the world among us and to be the only things awake. The wind, high and boisterous but now, has died away and hoarsely mutters in its sleep.

Exercise 35
Holding My Breath
From *Robinson Crusoe* by Daniel DeFoe

The wave that came upon me again buried me at once twenty or thirty feet deep in its own body, and I could feel myself carried with a mighty force and swiftness towards the shore—a very great way; but I held my breath and assisted myself to swim still forward with all my might. I was ready to burst with holding my breath, when, as I felt myself rising up, so, to my immediate relief, I found my head and hands shoot out above the surface of the water; and though it was not two seconds of time that I could keep myself so, yet it relieved me greatly, gave me breath and new courage.

Weeds of Falsehood
From *The Life of Jesus Christ for the Young* by Richard Newton

Some time ago a little boy told his first falsehood. It was like a solitary little thistle seed, sown in the mellow soil of his heart. No eye but that of God saw him as he planted it. But it sprang up—O, how quickly! and in a little time another seed dropped from it into the ground, and then another, and another, each in its turn bearing more and more of those troublesome thistles. And now his heart is like a field of which the weeds have taken entire possession. It is as difficult for him to speak the truth as it is for the gardener to clear his land of the ugly thistles that have once gained a rooting in the soil.

Out of Doors
From *Emma* by Jane Austen

The weather continued much the same all the following morning; and the same loneliness and the same melancholy seemed to reign at Hartfield; but in the afternoon it cleared; the wind changed into a softer quarter; the clouds were carried off; the sun appeared; it was summer again. With all the eagerness which such a transition gives, Emma resolved to be out of doors as soon as possible. Never had the exquisite sight, smell, sensation of nature—tranquil, warm, and brilliant after a storm—been more attractive to her. She longed for the serenity they might gradually introduce.

Some Brief Memory
From *Oliver Twist* by Charles Dickens

The boy stirred and smiled in his sleep, as though these marks of pity and compassion had awakened some pleasant dream of a love and affection he had never known. Thus, a strain of gentle music or the rippling of water in a silent place or the odor of a flower or the mention of a familiar word will sometimes call up sudden dim remembrances of scenes that never were in this life; which vanish like a breath; which some brief memory of a happier existence, long gone by, would seem to have awakened; which no voluntary exertion of the mind can ever recall.

Equidistant Pennies
From *Amusements in Mathematics* by Henry Ernest Dudeney

Here is a really hard puzzle, and yet its conditions are so absurdly simple. Every reader knows how to place four pennies so that they are equidistant from each other. All you have to do is to arrange three of them flat on the table so that they touch one another in the form of a triangle, and lay the fourth penny on top in the center. Then, as every penny touches every other penny, they are all at equal distances from one another. Now try to do the same thing with five pennies—place them so that every penny shall touch every other penny—and you will find it a different matter altogether.

The Haircut
From *Emma* by Jane Austen

Emma's very good opinion of Frank Churchill was a little shaken the following day by hearing that he was gone off to London merely to have his hair cut. A sudden freak seemed to have seized him at breakfast, and he had sent for a chaise and set off, intending to return to dinner, but with no more important view that appeared than having his hair cut. There was certainly no harm in his traveling sixteen miles twice over on such an errand; but there was an air of foppery and nonsense in it which she could not approve. It did not accord with the rationality of plan, the moderation in expense, or even the unselfish warmth of heart which she had believed herself to discern in him yesterday.

Trapping Words
From *The Story of My Life* by Helen Keller

I had now the key to all language, and I was eager to learn to use it. Children who hear, acquire language without any particular effort; the words that fall from others' lips they catch on the wing, as it were, delightedly, while the little deaf child must trap them by a slow and often painful process. But whatever the process, the result is wonderful. Gradually from naming an object we advance step by step until we have traversed the vast distance between our first stammered syllable and the sweep of thought in a line of Shakespeare.

Nature
By Henry Wadsworth Longfellow

As a fond mother, when the day is over,
Leads by the hand her little child to bed,
Half willing, half reluctant to be led,
And leave his broken playthings on the floor,
Still gazing at them through the open door,
Nor wholly reassured and comforted
By promises of others in their stead,
Which, though more splendid, may not please him more;
So Nature deals with us, and takes away
Our playthings one by one, and by the hand
Leads us to rest so gently, that we go
Scarce knowing if we wish to go or stay,
Being too full of sleep to understand
How far the unknown transcends the what we know.

Fogg's Riches
From *Around the World in Eighty Days* by Jules Verne

Was Phileas Fogg rich? Undoubtedly. But those who knew him best could not imagine how he had made his fortune, and Mr. Fogg was the last person to whom to apply for the information. He was not lavish, nor, on the contrary, avaricious; for whenever he knew that money was needed for a noble, useful, or benevolent purpose, he supplied it quietly and sometimes anonymously. He was, in short, the least communicative of men. He talked very little and seemed all the more mysterious for his taciturn manner. His daily habits were quite open to observation; but whatever he did was so exactly the same thing that he had always done before, that the wits of the curious were fairly puzzled.

Exercise 44
The Order of the Houses
From *The Adventures of Sherlock Holmes* by Sir Arthur Conan Doyle

---

"Let me see," said Holmes, standing at the corner and glancing along the line, "I should like just to remember the order of the houses here. It is a hobby of mine to have an exact knowledge of London. There is Mortimer's, the tobacconist, the little newspaper shop, the Coburg branch of the City and Suburban Bank, the Vegetarian Restaurant, and McFarlane's carriage-building depot. That carries us right on to the other block. And now, Doctor, we've done our work, so it's time we had some play. A sandwich and a cup of coffee and then off to violin-land, where all is sweetness and delicacy and harmony, and there are no red-headed clients to vex us with their conundrums."

Exercise 45
Toothbrush and Nailbrush
From *Letters of Franz Liszt* by Franz Liszt

I thank you most truly for the kindness which you have shown to B. He is in many things somewhat awkward, impractical, and almost looks as though he could not devote himself to any productive and consistently carried-out form of activity. Nonetheless is there in him a certain capacity and worth which, in a somewhat more regular position than he has yet been able to attain, would make him appear worth more. A more frequent application of a few utensils, such as soak toothbrush and nailbrush, might also be recommended to him! I expect much good to result from your influence on B's further work and fortunes and hope that your store of patience will not be too sorely tried by him.

With heartfelt greetings, your

F. Liszt

Harvest on the Island
From *Robinson Crusoe* by Daniel DeFoe

It was now harvest and our crop in good order. It was not the most plentiful increase I had seen in the island, but however, it was enough to answer our end; for from twenty-two bushels of barley we brought in and thrashed out above two hundred and twenty bushels, and the like in proportion of the rice, which was store enough for our food to the next harvest though all the sixteen Spaniards had been on shore with me; or if we had been ready for a voyage, it would very plentifully have victualled our ship to have carried us to any part of the world, that is to say, any part of America.

The Bicycle Salesman
From *Amusements in Mathematics* by Henry Ernest Dudeney

Here is a little tangle that is perpetually cropping up in various guises. A cyclist bought a bicycle for L15 and gave in payment a check for L25. The seller went to a neighboring shopkeeper and got him to change the check for him, and the cyclist, having received his L10 change, mounted the machine and disappeared. The check proved to be valueless, and the salesman was requested by his neighbor to refund the amount he had received. To do this, he was compelled to borrow the L25 from a friend, as the cyclist forgot to leave his address and could not be found. Now, as the bicycle cost the salesman L11, how much money did he lose altogether?

Exercise 48
The Hat
From *The Adventures of Sherlock Holmes* by Sir Arthur Conan Doyle

I had called upon my friend Sherlock Holmes upon the second morning after Christmas with the intention of wishing him the compliments of the season. He was lounging upon the sofa in a purple dressing-gown, a pipe-rack within his reach upon the right and a pile of crumpled morning papers, evidently newly studied, near at hand. Beside the couch was a wooden chair, and on the angle of the back hung a very seedy and disreputable hard-felt hat, much the worse for wear and cracked in several places. A lens and a forceps lying upon the seat of the chair suggested that the hat had been suspended in this manner for the purpose of examination.

Exercise 49
Deduce
From *The Adventures of Sherlock Holmes* by Sir Arthur Conan Doyle

"He brought round both hat and goose to me on Christmas morning, knowing that even the smallest problems are of interest to me. The goose we retained until this morning, when there were signs that, in spite of the slight frost, it would be well that it should be eaten without unnecessary delay. Its finder has carried it off, therefore, to fulfill the ultimate destiny of a goose, while I continue to retain the hat of the unknown gentleman who lost his Christmas dinner."

"Did he not advertise?"

"No."

"Then what clue could you have as to his identity?"

"Only as much as we can deduce."

"From his hat?"

"Precisely."

Exercise 50
Changes
From *Mansfield Park* by Jane Austen

"This is pretty, very pretty," said Fanny, looking around her as they were thus sitting together one day. "Every time I come into this shrubbery I am more struck with its growth and beauty. Three years ago this was nothing but a rough hedgerow along the upper side of the field, never thought of as anything or capable of becoming anything; and now it is converted into a walk, and it would be difficult to say whether most valuable as a convenience or an ornament; and perhaps in another three years, we may be forgetting—almost forgetting what it was before. How wonderful, how very wonderful the operations of time and the changes of the human mind!"

Good Company
From *Letters of Franz Liszt* by Franz Liszt

To Alphonse Brot in Paris:

It would give us great pleasure, my dear M. Brot, if you would come and dine with us without ceremony tomorrow, Monday, about 6 o'clock. I do not promise you a good dinner—that is not the business of us poor artists—but the good company you will meet will, I trust, make up for that. Monsieur Hugo [the poet] and Edgard Quinet [French writer and philosopher] have promised to come. So do try not to disappoint us, for we should miss you much. My good mother told me to press you to come, for she is very fond of you. Till tomorrow then! Kind regards and thanks.

F. Liszt

To a Skylark
By William Wordsworth

Ethereal minstrel! pilgrim of the sky!
Dost thou despise the earth where cares abound?
Or, while the wings aspire, are heart and eye
Both with thy nest upon the dewy ground?
Thy nest which thou canst drop into at will,
Those quivering wings composed, that music still!

Leave to the nightingale her shady wood;
A privacy of glorious light is thine;
Whence thou dost pour upon the world a flood
Of harmony, with instinct more divine;
Type of the wise who soar, but never roam;
True to the kindred points of Heaven and Home!

A New Coat for Father
From *Pinocchio* by Carlo Collodi

See Pinocchio hurrying off to school with his new A-B-C book under his arm! As he walked along, his brain was busy planning hundreds of wonderful things, building hundreds of castles in the air. Talking to himself, he said, "In school today I'll learn to read, tomorrow to write, and the day after tomorrow I'll do arithmetic. Then, clever as I am, I can earn a lot of money. With the very first pennies I make, I'll buy Father a new cloth coat. Cloth, did I say? No, it shall be of gold and silver with diamond buttons. That poor man certainly deserves it; for, after all, isn't he in his shirtsleeves because he was good enough to buy a book for me? On this cold day, too! Fathers are indeed good to their children!"

Exercise 54
Out of a Cave
From *Robinson Crusoe* by Daniel DeFoe

It continued raining all that night and great part of the next day, so that I could not stir abroad; but my mind being more composed, I began to think of what I had best do; concluding that if the island was subject to these earthquakes, there would be no living for me in a cave, but I must consider of building a little hut in an open place which I might surround with a wall, as I had done here, and so make myself secure from wild beasts or men; for I concluded, if I stayed where I was, I should certainly one time or other be buried alive.

Exercise 55
Admire the Scenery
From *The Adventures of Sherlock Holmes* by Sir Arthur Conan Doyle

By eleven o'clock the next day we were well upon our way to the old English capital. Holmes had been buried in the morning papers all the way down, but after we had passed the Hampshire border he threw them down and began to admire the scenery. It was an ideal spring day—a light blue sky flecked with little fleecy white clouds drifting across from west to east. The sun was shining very brightly, and yet there was an exhilarating nip in the air, which set an edge to a man's energy. All over the countryside, away to the rolling hills around Aldershot, the little red and gray roofs of the farmsteads peeped out from amid the light green of the new foliage.

The Skipping-Rope
From *The Secret Garden* by Frances Hodgson Burnett

The skipping-rope was a wonderful thing. She counted and skipped, and skipped and counted, until her cheeks were quite red and she was more interested than she had ever been since she was born. The sun was shining and a little wind was blowing—not a rough wind, but one which came in delightful little gusts and brought a fresh scent of newly turned earth with it. She skipped round the fountain garden and up one walk and down another. She skipped at last into the kitchen garden and saw Ben Weatherstaff digging and talking to his robin, which was hopping about him. She skipped down the walk toward him, and he lifted his head and looked at her with a curious expression. She had wondered if he would notice her. She wanted him to see her skip.

Hot on the Trail

From *The Adventures of Sherlock Holmes* by Sir Arthur Conan Doyle

Sherlock Holmes was transformed when he was hot upon such a scent as this. Men who had only known the quiet thinker and logician of Baker Street would have failed to recognize him. His face flushed and darkened. His brows were drawn into two hard black lines, while his eyes shone out from beneath them with a steely glitter. His face was bent downward, his shoulders bowed, his lips compressed, and the veins stood out like whipcord in his long, sinewy neck. His nostrils seemed to dilate with a purely animal lust for the chase, and his mind was so absolutely concentrated upon the matter before him that a question or remark fell unheeded upon his ears, or at the most, only provoked a quick, impatient snarl in reply.

Exercise 58
Looking for Boats
From *Robinson Crusoe* by Daniel DeFoe

After I had thus laid the scheme of my design and in my imagination put it in practice, I continually made my tour every morning to the top of the hill, which was from my castle, as I called it, about three miles or more, to see if I could observe any boats upon the sea coming near the island or standing over towards it; but I began to tire of this hard duty after I had for two or three months constantly kept my watch but came always back without any discovery—there having not, in all that time, been the least appearance not only on or near the shore, but on the whole ocean so far as my eye or glass could reach every way.

Exercise 59
Thunderstorm
From *The Old Curiosity Shop* by Charles Dickens

It had been gradually getting overcast, and now the sky was dark and lowering, save where the glory of the departing sun piled up masses of gold and burning fire, decaying embers of which gleamed here and there through the black veil and shone redly down upon the earth. The wind began to moan in hollow murmurs as the sun went down, carrying glad day elsewhere, and a train of dull clouds coming up against it menaced thunder and lightning. Large drops of rain soon began to fall, and as the storm clouds came sailing onward, others supplied the void they left behind and spread over all the sky. Then was heard the low rumbling of distant thunder, then the lightning quivered, and then the darkness of an hour seemed to have gathered in an instant.

A Suit of Clothes
From *Robinson Crusoe* by Daniel DeFoe

I have mentioned that I saved the skins of all the creatures that I killed—I mean four-footed ones—and I had them hung up, stretched out with sticks in the sun, by which means some of them were so dry and hard that they were fit for little, but others were very useful. The first thing I made of these was a great cap for my head, with the hair on the outside to shoot off the rain; and this I performed so well that after, I made me a suit of clothes wholly of these skins—that is to say, a waistcoat, and breeches open at the knees, and both loose, for they were rather wanting to keep me cool than to keep me warm. I must not omit to acknowledge that they were wretchedly made, for if I was a bad carpenter, I was a worse tailor.

Exercise 61
August
From *The Pickwick Papers* by Charles Dickens

There is no month in the whole year in which nature wears a more beautiful appearance than in the month of August. Spring has many beauties, and May is a fresh and blooming month, but the charms of this time of year are enhanced by their contrast with the winter season. August has no such advantage. It comes when we remember nothing but clear skies, green fields, and sweet-smelling flowers—when the recollection of snow and ice and bleak winds has faded from our minds as completely as they have disappeared from the earth—and yet what a pleasant time it is! Orchards and cornfields ring with the hum of labor; trees bend beneath the thick clusters of rich fruit which bow their branches to the ground; and the corn, piled in graceful sheaves or waving in every light breath that sweeps above it, as if it wooed the sickle, tinges the landscape with a golden hue.

Exercise 62
Statue of a Frenchman
From *Swinton's Advanced Fourth Reader*

Standing among the trees in the little park named Union Square in the city of New York, is a bronze statue representing a tall young man in the close-fitting uniform of an American general of the time of the Revolution. With his right hand he clasps a sword to his breast; his left is stretched out toward a noble equestrian statue of Washington, which stands hard by.

This is the statue of a gallant young Frenchman who devoted his sword and his fortune to the cause of American liberty, and whose memory is kept green in the name of many a street and city and county in the land which he helped to make free. It is the statue of Lafayette.

Spelling Wisdom, Book Three, 80

Composed Upon Westminster Bridge
By William Wordsworth

Earth has not anything to show more fair:
Dull would he be of soul who could pass by
A sight so touching in its majesty:
This City now doth like a garment wear

The beauty of the morning: silent, bare,
Ships, towers, domes, theaters, and temples lie
Open unto the fields, and to the sky,
All bright and glittering in the smokeless air.

Never did sun more beautifully steep
In his first splendor valley, rock, or hill;
Never saw I, never felt, a calm so deep!

The river glideth at his own sweet will:
Dear God! the very houses seem asleep;
And all that mighty heart is lying still!

A Good Pastry Cook
From *Robinson Crusoe* by Daniel DeFoe

When the firewood was burned pretty much into embers or live coals, I drew them forward upon this hearth, so as to cover it all over, and there I let them lie till the hearth was very hot. Then sweeping away all the embers, I set down my loaf or loaves, and whelming down the earthen pot upon them, drew the embers all round the outside of the pot to keep in and add to the heat; and thus, as well as in the best oven in the world, I baked my barley-loaves and became in little time a good pastry cook into the bargain; for I made myself several cakes and puddings of the rice; but I made no pies, neither had I anything to put into them supposing I had, except the flesh either of fowls or goats.

Paramount Importance

From *The Adventures of Sherlock Holmes* by Sir Arthur Conan Doyle

My Dear Mr. Sherlock Holmes:

Lord Backwater tells me that I may place implicit reliance upon your judgment and discretion. I have determined, therefore, to call upon you and to consult you in reference to the very painful event which has occurred in connection with my wedding. Mr. Lestrade of Scotland Yard is acting already in the matter, but he assures me that he sees no objection to your cooperation and that he even thinks that it might be of some assistance. I will call at four o'clock in the afternoon, and should you have any other engagement at that time, I hope that you will postpone it as this matter is of paramount importance.

Yours faithfully,
St. Simon

Progress and Guessing
From *The Story of My Life* by Helen Keller

My progress in lip-reading and speech was not what my teachers and I had hoped and expected it would be. It was my ambition to speak like other people, and my teachers believed that this could be accomplished; but although we worked hard and faithfully, yet we did not quite reach our goal. I suppose we aimed too high, and disappointment was therefore inevitable. I still regarded arithmetic as a system of pitfalls. I hung about the dangerous frontier of "guess," avoiding with infinite trouble to myself and others, the broad valley of reason. When I was not guessing, I was jumping at conclusions, and this fault, in addition to my dullness, aggravated my difficulties more than was right or necessary.

God Employs Little Things
From *The Life of Jesus Christ for the Young* by Richard Newton

Look at yonder sun. God made it and hung it up there in the sky that it might give light to our world. But the light which this sun gives comes to us in tiny little bits, smaller than the point of the finest needle that ever was made. They are so small that hundreds of them can rush right into our eyes, as they are doing all the time, and not hurt them the least. Here we see how God makes use of little things and does a great work with them.

And then look at yonder ocean. The waves of that ocean are so powerful that they can break in pieces the strongest ships that men have ever built. And yet, when God wishes to keep that mighty ocean in its place, he makes use of little grains of sand for this purpose. Here again we see how God employs little things and does a great work with them.

Exercise 68
Agree in Number

Now I want to remind you of a key grammar rule that many people forget—even adults. The rule is this: a pronoun should agree in number with the noun it may replace. It sounds somewhat intimidating, but it really is easy if you only think about it.

Take, for an example, this sentence: "If your child is doing well, praise them." You can see that "them" renames "child." Yet, "them" is a plural word, meaning more than one person; "child" is a singular word, meaning only one person. The two numbers disagree.

How much better to say, "If your children are doing well, praise them," or "If your child is doing well, praise him!" Keep this simple rule in mind and you will reduce your grammatical errors.

Exercise 69
Thanks for the Harvest
By Laura Ingalls Wilder

The season is over, the rush and struggle of growing and saving the crops is past for another year, and the time has come when we pause and reverently give thanks for the harvest. For it is not to our efforts alone that our measure of success is due, but to the life principle in the earth and the seed, to the sunshine and to the rain—to the goodness of God.

We may not be altogether satisfied with the year's results, and we can do a terrific amount of grumbling when we take the notion. But I am sure we all know in our hearts that we have a great deal for which to be thankful. In spite of disappointment and weariness and perhaps sorrow, His goodness and mercy does follow us all the days of our lives.

Exercise 70
The Ocean Course
From *Twenty Thousand Leagues Under the Sea* by Jules Verne

"Well," said Conseil, "after all this, are we going right?"

"Yes," I replied, "for we are going the way of the sun, and here the sun is in the north."

"No doubt," said Ned Land, "but it remains to be seen whether he will bring the ship into the Pacific or the Atlantic Ocean, that is, into frequented or deserted seas."

I could not answer that question, and I feared that Captain Nemo would rather take us to the vast ocean that touches the coasts of Asia and America at the same time. He would thus complete the tour round the submarine world and return to those waters in which the Nautilus could sail freely. We ought, before long, to settle this important point. The Nautilus went at a rapid pace. The polar circle was soon passed, and the course shaped for Cape Horn.

Exercise 71
Journey Mercies
From *The Life and Diary of David Brainerd* by Jonathan Edwards, ed.

This day rode home to my own house and people. The poor Indians appeared very glad of my return. Found my house and all things in safety. I presently fell on my knees and blessed God for my safe return after a long and tedious journey and a season of sickness in several places where I had been, and after I had been ill myself. God has renewed His kindness to me in preserving me one journey more. I have taken many considerable journeys since this time last year, and yet God has never suffered one of my bones to be broken or any distressing calamity to befall me, often exposed to cold and hunger in the wilderness where the comforts of life were not to be had; have frequently been lost in the woods; and sometimes obliged to ride much of the night; and once lay out in the woods all night. Yet, blessed be God, He has preserved me!

Courteous to Aunts
From *Little Women* by Louisa May Alcott

Gentlemen, which means boys, be courteous to the old maids, no matter how poor and plain and prim, for the only chivalry worth having is that which is the readiest to pay deference to the old, protect the feeble, and serve womankind, regardless of rank, age, or color. Just recollect the good aunts who have not only lectured and fussed, but nursed and petted, too often without thanks—the scrapes they have helped you out of, the tips they have given you from their small store, the stitches the patient old fingers have set for you, the steps the willing old feet have taken—and gratefully pay the dear old ladies the little attentions that women love to receive as long as they live. The bright-eyed girls are quick to see such traits and will like you all the better for them, and if death, almost the only power that can part mother and son, should rob you of yours, you will be sure to find a tender welcome and maternal cherishing from some Aunt Priscilla, who has kept the warmest corner of her lonely old heart for "the best nevvy in the world."

Breathes There the Man

By Sir Walter Scott

Breathes there the man, with soul so dead,
Who never to himself hath said,
This is my own, my native land!
Whose heart hath never within him burned,
As home his footsteps he hath turned
From wandering on a foreign strand?
If such there breathe, go mark him well:
For him no minstrel raptures swell;
High though his titles, proud his name,
Boundless his wealth as wish can claim;
Despite those titles, power, and pelf,
The wretch, concentered all in self,
Living, shall forfeit fair renown,
And, doubly dying, shall go down
To the vile dust from whence he sprung,
Unwept, unhonored, and unsung.

Why Is the World So Beautiful if Not for Us?
By Laura Ingalls Wilder

King Winter has sent warning of his coming! There was a delightful freshness in the air the other morning, and all over the low places lay the first frost of the season.

What a beautiful world this is! Have you noticed the wonderful coloring of the sky at sunrise? For me there is no time like the early morning, when the spirit of light broods over the earth at its awakening. What glorious colors in the woods these days! Did you ever think that great painters have spent their lives trying to reproduce on canvas what we may see every day?

Thousands of dollars are paid for their pictures which are not so beautiful as those nature gives us freely. The colors in the sky at sunset, the delicate tints of the early spring foliage, the brilliant autumn leaves, the softly-colored grasses and lovely flowers—what painter ever equaled their beauties with paint and brush?

Love of Money

My Dear Son,

I want to congratulate you on your receipt of such a large sum of money. But at the same time I want to warn you of the damage that the love of money can do to a man. I have seen greed change a man's character. It seems not to matter whether he has one hundred or one billion dollars, the lust for more begins to tempt him. He will cheat in order to increase his store; he will bribe in order to control those around him. His family will accustom themselves to expensive living, no longer content with their former wage.

I say all this not to discourage you, but to open your eyes to a potential threat that might hinder you from becoming the man you were raised to be. Keep money in its place and use it for good purposes, my son. You know what is right; don't let riches confuse you.

Your Loving Father

Exercise 76
First Thing in The Morning
From *The Practice of Piety* by Lewis Bayly

As soon as ever thou awakest in the morning, keep the door of thy heart fast shut, that no earthly thought may enter before that God come in first; and let him, before all others, have the first place there. So all evil thoughts either will not dare to come in or shall the easier be kept out; and the heart will more savor of piety and godliness all the day after; but if thy heart be not, at thy first waking, filled with some meditations of God and his word and dressed, like the lamp in the tabernacle, every morning and evening with the oil-olive of God's word and perfumed with the sweet incense of prayer, Satan will attempt to fill it with worldly cares or fleshly desires, so that it will grow unfit for the service of God all the day after, sending forth nothing but the stench of corrupt and lying words and of rash and blasphemous thoughts.

The Name on the Shield
From *The Life of Jesus Christ for the Young* by Richard Newton

Men have been very ingenious in trying to find out ways by which their names might be remembered among men when they themselves have passed away. The story is told of a soldier in ancient times who wished to preserve his name in some way. In order to do this, he engaged a celebrated artist to make him a shield and to work his name into the material of which the shield was composed in such a way that the name could not be taken out without destroying the shield. It was done. The soldier carried that shield bravely with him through many a hard-fought battle, feeling proud to think that his name was made so enduring. But that soldier is gone; his shield is gone; the artist who made it is gone; and no one knows the name that was wrought into that shield, nor the name of the artist who did the work.

Exercise 78
Day of the Week
From *Amusements in Mathematics* by Henry Ernest Dudeney

A facetious individual who was taking a long walk in the country came upon a yokel sitting on a stile. As the gentleman was not quite sure of his road, he thought he would make inquiries of the local inhabitant; but at the first glance he jumped too hastily to the conclusion that he had dropped on the village idiot. He therefore decided to test the fellow's intelligence by first putting to him the simplest question he could think of, which was, "What day of the week is this, my good man?" The following is the smart answer that he received:

"When the day after tomorrow is yesterday, today will be as far from Sunday as today was from Sunday when the day before yesterday was tomorrow."

Can the reader say what day of the week it was? It is pretty evident that the countryman was not such a fool as he looked. The gentleman went on his road a puzzled but a wiser man.

The Grindstone

From *Robinson Crusoe* by Daniel DeFoe

The next morning I began to consider of means to put this resolve into execution; but I was at a great loss about my tools. I had three large axes and abundance of hatchets (for we carried the hatchets for traffic with the Indians); but with much chopping and cutting knotty hard wood, they were all full of notches and dull; and though I had a grindstone, I could not turn it and grind my tools too. This cost me as much thought as a statesman would have bestowed upon a grand point of politics or a judge upon the life and death of a man. At length I contrived a wheel with a string, to turn it with my foot, that I might have both my hands at liberty. Note: I had never seen any such thing in England, or at least, not to take notice how it was done, though since, I have observed it is very common there; besides that, my grindstone was very large and heavy. This machine cost me a full week's work to bring it to perfection.

Exercise 80
Horse Owners
From *Black Beauty* by Anna Sewell

My master often drove me in double harness with my mother, because she was steady and could teach me how to go better than a strange horse. She told me the better I behaved, the better I should be treated, and that it was wisest always to do my best to please my master. "But," said she, "there are a great many kinds of men; there are good thoughtful men like our master, that any horse may be proud to serve; and there are bad, cruel men, who never ought to have a horse or dog to call their own. Besides, there are a great many foolish men, vain, ignorant, and careless, who never trouble themselves to think; these spoil more horses than all, just for want of sense; they don't mean it, but they do it for all that. I hope you will fall into good hands; but a horse never knows who may buy him or who may drive him; it is all a chance for us; but still I say, do your best wherever it is and keep up your good name."

What the Sun Saw
From *Little Women* by Louisa May Alcott

When the sun peeped into the girls' room early next morning to promise them a fine day, he saw a comical sight. Each had made such preparation for the fete as seemed necessary and proper. Meg had an extra row of little curlpapers across her forehead, Jo had copiously anointed her afflicted face with cold cream, Beth had taken Joanna to bed with her to atone for the approaching separation, and Amy had capped the climax by putting a clothespin on her nose to uplift the offending feature. It was one of the kind artists use to hold the paper on their drawing boards, therefore quite appropriate and effective for the purpose it was now being put. This funny spectacle appeared to amuse the sun, for he burst out with such radiance that Jo woke up and roused her sisters by a hearty laugh at Amy's ornament.

Rip Van Winkle's Dog
From *The Sketch Book* by Washington Irving

Rip's sole domestic adherent was his dog Wolf, who was as much henpecked as his master; for Dame Van Winkle regarded them as companions in idleness and even looked upon Wolf with an evil eye as the cause of his master's going so often astray. True it is, in all points of spirit befitting in honorable dog, he was as courageous an animal as ever scoured the woods; but what courage can withstand the evil-doing and all-besetting terrors of a woman's tongue? The moment Wolf entered the house his crest fell, his tail drooped to the ground or curled between his legs, he sneaked about with a gallows air, casting many a sidelong glance at Dame Van Winkle, and at the least flourish of a broomstick or ladle, he would fly to the door with yelping precipitation.

Daffodils
By William Wordsworth

I wandered lonely as a cloud
That floats on high over vales and hills,
When all at once I saw a crowd,
A host of golden daffodils;
Beside the lake, beneath the trees,
Fluttering and dancing in the breeze.

Continuous as the stars that shine
And twinkle on the milky way,
They stretched in never-ending line
Along the margin of a bay:
Ten thousand saw I at a glance,
Tossing their heads in sprightly dance.

The waves beside them danced, but they
Out-did the sparkling waves in glee:
A poet could not but be gay
In such a jocund company:
I gazed and gazed but little thought
What wealth the show to me had brought:

For oft when on my couch I lie
In vacant or in pensive mood,
They flash upon that inward eye
Which is the bliss of solitude,
And then my heart with pleasure fills,
And dances with the daffodils.

Exercise 84
The Building
From *The Adventures of Sherlock Holmes* by Sir Arthur Conan Doyle

---

The building was of gray, lichen-blotched stone with a high central portion and two curving wings, like the claws of a crab, thrown out on each side. In one of these wings the windows were broken and blocked with wooden boards, while the roof was partly caved in, a picture of ruin. The central portion was in little better repair, but the right-hand block was comparatively modern, and the blinds in the windows, with the blue smoke curling up from the chimneys, showed that this was where the family resided. Some scaffolding had been erected against the end wall, and the stonework had been broken into, but there were no signs of any workmen at the moment of our visit. Holmes walked slowly up and down the ill-trimmed lawn and examined with deep attention the outsides of the windows.

Forego and Give Up

From *The Life and Diary of David Brainerd* by Jonathan Edwards, ed.

God has made me willing to do anything that I can do, consistent with truth, for the sake of peace, and that I might not be a stumbling block to others. For this reason I can cheerfully forego and give up what I verily believe, after the most mature and impartial search, is my right, in some instances. God has given me that disposition that, if this were the case that a man has done me an hundred injuries and I (though ever so much provoked to it) have done him one, I feel disposed and heartily willing humbly to confess my fault to him and on my knees to ask forgiveness of him; though at the same time he should justify himself in all the injuries he has done me and should only make use of my humble confession to blacken my character the more and represent me as the only person guilty.

Mr. Morgan G. Bloomgarten, the millionaire, known in the States as the Clam King, had, for his sins, more money than he knew what to do with. It bored him. So he determined to persecute some of his poor but happy friends with it. They had never done him any harm, but he resolved to inoculate them with the "source of all evil." He therefore proposed to distribute a million dollars among them and watch them go rapidly to the bad. But he was a man of strange fancies and superstitions, and it was an inviolable rule with him never to make a gift that was not either one dollar or some power of seven—such as 7, 49, 343, 2,401, which numbers of dollars are produced by simply multiplying sevens together. Another rule of his was that he would never give more than six persons exactly the same sum. Now, how was he to distribute the 1,000,000 dollars? You may distribute the money among as many people as you like under the conditions given.

Blessed is he whose transgression is forgiven, whose sin is covered.
Blessed is the man unto whom the Lord imputeth not iniquity,
and in whose spirit there is no guile.
When I kept silence, my bones waxed old through my roaring all the day long.
For day and night thy hand was heavy upon me:
my moisture is turned into the drought of summer. Selah.

I acknowledged my sin unto thee, and mine iniquity have I not hid.
I said, I will confess my transgressions unto the Lord;
and thou forgavest the iniquity of my sin. Selah.

For this shall every one that is godly pray unto thee
in a time when thou mayest be found:
surely in the floods of great waters they shall not come nigh unto him.
Thou art my hiding place;
thou shalt preserve me from trouble;
thou shalt compass me about with songs of deliverance. Selah.

I will instruct thee and teach thee in the way which thou shalt go:
I will guide thee with mine eye.
Be ye not as the horse, or as the mule,
which have no understanding:
whose mouth must be held in with bit and bridle,
lest they come near unto thee.
Many sorrows shall be to the wicked:
but he that trusteth in the Lord, mercy shall compass him about.
Be glad in the Lord, and rejoice, ye righteous:
and shout for joy, all ye that are upright in heart.

Mud Spatters

From *The Adventures of Sherlock Holmes* by Sir Arthur Conan Doyle

"You must not fear," said he soothingly, bending forward and patting her forearm. "We shall soon set matters right, I have no doubt. You have come in by train this morning, I see."

"You know me, then?"

"No, but I observe the second half of a return ticket in the palm of your left glove. You must have started early, and yet you had a good drive in a dog-cart along heavy roads before you reached the station."

The lady gave a violent start and stared in bewilderment at my companion.

"There is no mystery, my dear madam," said he, smiling. "The left arm of your jacket is spattered with mud in no less than seven places. The marks are perfectly fresh. There is no vehicle save a dog-cart which throws up mud in that way, and then only when you sit on the left-hand side of the driver."

Provisions
From *Robinson Crusoe* by Daniel DeFoe

But this was not all; for now I not only had goat's flesh to feed on when I pleased, but milk too—a thing which, indeed, in the beginning I did not so much as think of, and which, when it came into my thoughts, was really an agreeable surprise, for now I set up my dairy and had sometimes a gallon or two of milk in a day. And as Nature, who gives supplies of food to every creature, dictates even naturally how to make use of it, so I, that had never milked a cow, much less a goat, or seen butter or cheese made only when I was a boy, after a great many essays and miscarriages, made both butter and cheese at last, also salt (though I found it partly made to my hand by the heat of the sun upon some of the rocks of the sea), and never wanted it afterwards. How mercifully can our Creator treat His creatures, even in those conditions in which they seemed to be overwhelmed in destruction! How can He sweeten the bitterest providences and give us cause to praise Him for dungeons and prisons! What a table was here spread for me in the wilderness, where I saw nothing at first but to perish for hunger!

Exercise 90
The Historian's Responsibility
By Theodore Parker

The historian is to tell of the origin of the people, of their rise, their decline, their fall and end. The causes which advanced or retarded the nation are to be sought and their actions explained. He is to inquire what sentiments and ideas prevailed in the nation; whence they came; how they organized, and with results. Hence not merely the civil and military transactions are to be looked after but the philosophy which prevails in the nation is to be ascertained—the literature, laws, and religion. The historian is to describe the industrial condition of the people, the state of agriculture, commerce, and the arts—both the useful and the beautiful. He must tell us of the social state of the people, the relation of the cultivator to the soil, the relation of class to class. It is well to know what songs the peasant sung; what prayers he prayed; what food he ate; what tools he wrought with; what tax he paid; how he stood connected with the soil; how he brought to war; and what weapons armed him for the fight.

Exercise 91
Robin Quarrels
From *Swinton's Advanced Fourth Reader*

The robin is one of our most familiar birds and often makes its nest close to a house, even on a pillar of the piazza. One pair built their nest for three summers in a basket suspended from the ceiling of my front piazza, where people were constantly coming and going.

During the winter in Florida, we often see immense flocks that have migrated from the north. At this time they live peaceably together; but in the spring when they return to their northern homes, all this is changed.

Now the males, which appear to be jealous of one another, have many fierce battles. One will pounce upon another, seemingly for no other reason than that he was singing his best and had attracted a female to listen to him. After they have chosen their mates and homes they are more peaceable, yet no two pairs can agree to build in the same tree.

Exercise 92
Robin Nests
From *Swinton's Advanced Fourth Reader*

A large spruce stands near my back door, and this spring two pairs of robins selected this tree in which to erect their domiciles. They could not agree to settle the matter quietly, but had many bitter contests over it. I could almost pick them up as they tumbled over the ground. It seemed a little strange that the females never joined in the fight, for they alone build the nest, the males never assisting them.

The conqueror's mate now proceeds to construct the nest in the chosen tree, while the other selects a spruce on the lawn at another side of the house. Although two robins cannot agree to build in the same tree, yet a brown thrush and a robin have made their homes not three feet apart on this tree at the back door, and both are now feeding their young and never have any quarrels.

Spelling Wisdom, Book Three, 110   *www.SimplyCharlotteMason.com*

Pliable Materials
From *Swinton's Advanced Fourth Reader*

I have large pans set in the earth, and these are kept filled with fresh water for the birds to bathe in. It was very dry while the robins were building, and when they collected the material for the nests they would take it to the bath-dishes and hold it in the water until it was well soaked. In this way it was rendered pliable, and the birds were able to work it in with the mud.

I found they were making sad havoc with some of my plants that had just been set out. They were after the moist earth; so I had a quantity of damp clay placed near one of the baths, and this they seemed to think much better, for they disturbed my plants no more.

Peace

By Henry Vaughan

My soul, there is a country
Far beyond the stars
Where stands a winged sentry
All skillful in the wars:
There, above noise and danger,
Sweet peace sits crowned with smiles,
And One born in a manger
Commands the beauteous files.
He is thy gracious friend,
And (O my soul, awake!)
Did in pure love descend
To die here for thy sake.
If thou canst get but thither,
There grows the flower of peace,
The rose that cannot wither,
Thy fortress, and thy ease.
Leave then thy foolish ranges;
For none can thee secure
But One, who never changes,
Thy God, thy life, thy cure.

Exercise 95
Influence for Good
From *The Life of Jesus Christ for the Young* by Richard Newton

---

There are twenty-one epistles in the New Testament. Of these, the apostle Paul wrote fourteen. They form a large part of the New Testament. Now suppose we could take these epistles of Paul, chapter by chapter, and follow every verse in each chapter as it has gone round the world from age to age and find out every case where good has been done to any soul, what a history we should have! No one could write such a history now. But I suppose we shall have such a history set before us when we get to Heaven. Then we shall understand better than we can do now how great the apostle Paul was in the influence for good which he exerted. But though none of us can be compared at all with this great man, yet if we are trying, like him, to love and serve the blessed Savior, we may all, even to the youngest, be exerting influences for good that will last forever.

First Night Stranded
From *The Swiss Family Robinson* by Johann Wyss

We should have been badly off without the shelter of our tent, for the night proved as cold as the day had been hot, but we managed to sleep comfortably, everyone being thoroughly fatigued by the labors of the day.

The voice of our vigilant cock, which as he loudly saluted the rising moon, was the last sound I heard at night, roused me at daybreak, and I then awoke my wife, that in the quiet interval while yet our children slept, we might take counsel together on our situation and prospects. It was plain to both of us that in the first place, we should ascertain if possible the fate of our late companions and then examine into the nature and resources of the country on which we were stranded.

Exercise 97
A Season of Prayer
From *The Life and Diary of David Brainerd* by Jonathan Edwards, ed.

In the evening I withdrew and enjoyed a happy season in secret prayer. God was pleased to give me the exercise of faith and, thereby, brought the invisible and eternal world near to my soul, which appeared sweetly to me. I hoped that my weary pilgrimage in the world would be short, and that it would not be long before I was brought to my heavenly home and Father's house. I was resigned to God's will, to tarry His time, to do His work, and suffer His pleasure. I felt thankfulness to God for all my pressing desertions of late; for I am persuaded they have been made a means of making me more humble and much more resigned. I felt pleased to be little, to be nothing, and to lie in the dust. I enjoyed life and consolation in pleading for the dear children of God and the kingdom of Christ in the world; and my soul earnestly breathed after holiness and the enjoyment of God. Oh, come, Lord Jesus, come quickly.

Barrels of Honey
From *Amusements in Mathematics* by Henry Ernest Dudeney

Once upon a time there was an aged merchant of Baghdad who was much respected by all who knew him. He had three sons, and it was a rule of his life to treat them all exactly alike. Whenever one received a present, the other two were each given one of equal value. One day this worthy man fell sick and died, bequeathing all his possessions to his three sons in equal shares.

The only difficulty that arose was over the stock of honey. There were exactly twenty-one barrels. The old man had left instructions that not only should every son receive an equal quantity of honey, but should receive exactly the same number of barrels, and that no honey should be transferred from barrel to barrel on account of the waste involved. Now, as seven of these barrels were full of honey, seven were half-full, and seven were empty, this was found to be quite a puzzle, especially as each brother objected to taking more than four barrels of the same description—full, half-full, or empty. Can you show how they succeeded in making a correct division of the property?

Exercise 99
The Footprint
From *Robinson Crusoe* by Daniel DeFoe

It happened one day about noon, going towards my boat, I was exceedingly surprised with the print of a man's naked foot on the shore, which was very plain to be seen on the sand. I stood like one thunderstruck or as if I had seen an apparition. I listened, I looked round me, but I could hear nothing nor see anything; I went up to a rising ground to look farther; I went up the shore and down the shore, but it was all one; I could see no other impression but that one. I went to it again to see if there were any more and to observe if it might not be my fancy; but there was no room for that, for there was exactly the print of a foot—toes, heel, and every part of a foot. How it came thither I knew not, nor could I in the least imagine; but after innumerable fluttering thoughts, like a man perfectly confused and out of myself, I came home to my fortification, not feeling, as we say, the ground I went on, but terrified to the last degree, looking behind me at every two or three steps, mistaking every bush and tree and fancying every stump at a distance to be a man.

Exercise 100
Poor Richard's Almanac
From *The Autobiography of Benjamin Franklin* by Benjamin Franklin

In 1732 I first published my Almanac under the name of Richard Saunders; it was continued by me about twenty-five years, commonly called Poor Richard's Almanac. I endeavored to make it both entertaining and useful, and it accordingly came to be in such demand that I reaped considerable profit from it, vending annually near ten thousand. And observing that it was generally read, scarce any neighborhood in the province being without it, I considered it as a proper vehicle for conveying instruction among the common people, who bought scarcely any other books; I therefore filled all the little spaces that occurred between the remarkable days in the calendar with proverbial sentences, chiefly such as inculcated industry and frugality as the means of procuring wealth and, thereby, securing virtue; it being more difficult for a man in want to act always honestly, as, to use here one of those proverbs, it is hard for an empty sack to stand upright.

Exercise 101
Condolences
By Abraham Lincoln

Executive Mansion
December 23, 1862

Dear Fanny:

It is with deep grief that I learn of the death of your kind and brave father, and especially, that it is affecting your young heart beyond what is common in such cases. In this sad world of ours, sorrow comes to all; and to the young, it comes with bitterest agony because it takes them unawares. The older have learned to ever expect it. I am anxious to afford some alleviation of your present distress. Perfect relief is not possible, except with time. You cannot now realize that you will ever feel better. Is not this so? And yet it is a mistake. You are sure to be happy again. To know this, which is certainly true, will make you some less miserable now. I have had experience enough to know what I say; and your dear father, instead of an agony, will yet be a sad sweet feeling in your heart of a purer and holier sort than you have known before.

Please present my kind regards to your afflicted mother.

Your sincere friend,
Abraham Lincoln

Stanley's Courage
From *Wonders of the Tropics* by Henry Davenport Northrop

No one can doubt that any man with less nerve and courage than Stanley would have turned back. Sitting in our quiet American homes, with all the evidences of civilization, peace, and comfort around us, it is impossible to fully realize the situation of the great explorer on this expedition, which had for its object the recovery of an explorer equally famous with himself. One thing was in Stanley's favor: all that money could afford was freely furnished, and his supplies were ample at the outset. Of course these supplies of clothing and other things necessary for exchange with the African tribes grew less as he advanced, but at this point of his journey he was still amply furnished.

Yet it must be remembered that Stanley was in a country which was very unhealthful—where there were many hostile tribes, where wars were constantly raging, where Arabs were in pursuit of their prey—and it was necessary for him to exercise all his ingenuity and show all his courage in overcoming difficulties and pushing forward in his great undertaking.

Exercise 103
Salvaging Iron
From *Robinson Crusoe* by Daniel DeFoe

The next day I made another voyage, and now, having plundered the ship of what was portable and fit to hand out, I began with the cables. Cutting the great cable into pieces such as I could move, I got two cables and a hawser on shore with all the ironwork I could get; and having cut down the spritsail-yard and the mizzen-yard and everything I could to make a large raft, I loaded it with all these heavy goods and came away. But my good luck began now to leave me; for this raft was so unwieldy and so overladen that after I had entered the little cove where I had landed the rest of my goods, not being able to guide it so handily as I did the other, it overset and threw me and all my cargo into the water. As for myself, it was no great harm, for I was near the shore; but as to my cargo, it was a great part of it lost, especially the iron, which I expected would have been of great use to me; however, when the tide was out I got most of the pieces of the cable ashore and some of the iron, though with infinite labor; for I was fain to dip for it into the water, a work which fatigued me very much. After this, I went every day on board and brought away what I could get.

Exercise 104
Home-Thoughts from Abroad
By Robert Browning

O, to be in England
Now that April's there,
And whoever wakes in England
Sees, some morning, unaware,
That the lowest boughs and the brushwood sheaf
Round the elm-tree bole are in tiny leaf,
While the chaffinch sings on the orchard bough
In England—now!

And after April, when May follows,
And the whitethroat builds, and all the swallows!
Hark, where my blossomed pear-tree in the hedge
Leans to the field and scatters on the clover
Blossoms and dewdrops—at the bent spray's edge—
That's the wise thrush; he sings each song twice over,
Lest you should think he never could recapture
The first fine careless rapture!
And though the fields look rough with hoary dew,
All will be gay when noontide wakes anew
The buttercups, the little children's dower
—Far brighter than this gaudy melon-flower!

Exercise 105
The Bell of Justice
From *Swinton's Advanced Fourth Reader*

There is a beautiful story that tells of a king in one of the old cities of Italy who caused a bell to be hung in a tower in one of the public squares and commanded that any one who had been wronged should ring the bell, when a judge would come to see that the person had his rights. This bell the king called the "Bell of Justice."

In the course of time the lower end of the bell rope rotted away, and a wild vine was tied to it to lengthen it. One day an old and starving horse that had been turned out by its owner to die, wandered into the town, and in trying to eat the vine, rang the bell.

The magistrate, coming to see who had rung, found the poor old horse tugging at the wild vine. Sending for the owner, he rebuked him sharply for his hardness of heart.

"What!" said he, "this faithful creature has toiled all its life for you, it has worn itself out in your service, and now when it is old you turn it out to starve? No, it shall not be! The poor beast has rung the bell of justice, and justice it shall have. I command you to give it proper food and shelter as long as it lives!"

Exercise 106
Nature Study
From *The Secret Garden* by Frances Hodgson Burnett

Colin saw it all, watching each change as it took place. Every morning he was brought out, and every hour of each day when it didn't rain he spent in the garden. Even gray days pleased him. He would lie on the grass "watching things growing," he said. If you watched long enough, he declared, you could see buds unsheath themselves. Also you could make the acquaintance of strange busy insect things running about on various unknown but evidently serious errands, sometimes carrying tiny scraps of straw or feather or food, or climbing blades of grass as if they were trees from whose tops one could look out to explore the country. A mole throwing up its mound at the end of its burrow and making its way out at last with the long-nailed paws which looked so like elfish hands, had absorbed him one whole morning. Ants' ways, beetles' ways, bees' ways, frogs' ways, birds' ways, plants' ways gave him a new world to explore, and when Dickon revealed them all and added foxes' ways, otters' ways, ferrets' ways, squirrels' ways, and trout and water-rats' and badgers' ways, there was no end to the things to talk about and think over.

Exercise 107
The Most Important Day
From *The Story of My Life* by Helen Keller

The most important day I remember in all my life is the one on which my teacher, Anne Mansfield Sullivan, came to me. I am filled with wonder when I consider the immeasurable contrasts between the two lives which it connects. It was the third of March, 1887, three months before I was seven years old.

On the afternoon of that eventful day, I stood on the porch, dumb, expectant. I guessed vaguely from my mother's signs and from the hurrying to and fro in the house that something unusual was about to happen, so I went to the door and waited on the steps. The afternoon sun penetrated the mass of honeysuckle that covered the porch, and fell on my upturned face. My fingers lingered almost unconsciously on the familiar leaves and blossoms which had just come forth to greet the sweet southern spring. I did not know what the future held of marvel or surprise for me. Anger and bitterness had preyed upon me continually for weeks, and a deep languor had succeeded this passionate struggle.

This thought ran long in my head and I was exceeding fond of it for some time, the pleasantness of the place tempting me; but when I came to a nearer view of it, I considered that I was now by the seaside where it was at least possible that something might happen to my advantage, and by the same ill fate that brought me hither, might bring some other unhappy wretches to the same place; and though it was scarce probable that any such thing should ever happen, yet to enclose myself among the hills and woods in the center of the island was to anticipate my bondage and to render such an affair not only improbable, but impossible; and that therefore I ought not by any means to remove. However, I was so enamored of this place that I spent much of my time there for the whole of the remaining part of the month of July; and though upon second thoughts, I resolved not to remove, yet I built me a little kind of a bower and surrounded it at a distance with a strong fence, being a double hedge as high as I could reach, well staked and filled between with brushwood; and here I lay very secure, sometimes two or three nights together, always going over it with a ladder; so that I fancied now I had my country house and my sea-coast house; and this work took me up to the beginning of August.

Exercise 109
Plans for Colin

From *The Secret Garden* by Frances Hodgson Burnett

The most absorbing thing, however, was the preparations to be made before Colin could be transported with sufficient secrecy to the garden. No one must see the chair-carriage and Dickon and Mary after they turned a certain corner of the shrubbery and entered upon the walk outside the ivied walls. As each day passed, Colin had become more and more fixed in his feeling that the mystery surrounding the garden was one of its greatest charms. Nothing must spoil that. No one must ever suspect that they had a secret. People must think that he was simply going out with Mary and Dickon because he liked them and did not object to their looking at him.

They had long and quite delightful talks about their route. They would go up this path and down that one and cross the other and go round among the fountain flowerbeds as if they were looking at the "bedding-out plants" the head gardener, Mr. Roach, had been having arranged. That would seem such a rational thing to do that no one would think it at all mysterious. They would turn into the shrubbery walks and lose themselves until they came to the long walls. It was almost as serious and elaborately thought out as the plans of march made by great generals in time of war.

Mercy on a Mouse
From *Swinton's Advanced Fourth Reader*

Alexander Wilson, the great lover and student of birds, relates a touching experience with a mouse. Here is the story in his own words: "One of my boys caught a mouse in school a few days ago and directly marched up to me with his prisoner. I set about drawing it that same evening; and all the while the pantings of its little heart showed that it was in the most extreme agonies of fear.

"I had intended to kill it, in order to fix it in the claws of a stuffed owl; but, happening to spill a few drops of water where it was tied, it lapped it up with such eagerness and looked up in my face with such an expression of supplicating terror, as perfectly overcame me.

"I immediately untied it and restored it to life and liberty. The agonies of a prisoner at the stake while the fire and instruments of torture are preparing could not be more severe than the sufferings of that poor mouse; and insignificant as the object was, I felt at that moment the sweet sensation that Mercy leaves on the mind when she triumphs over cruelty."

Exercise 111
Holman Hunt
From *Pictures Every Child Should Know* by Mary Schell Hoke Bacon

Holman Hunt was like most of his brother artists in all but his art. He hated school and at twelve years of age was taken from it. His father wanted him to become a warehouse merchant like himself, and he began life as clerk, or apprentice, to an auctioneer. He next went into the employment of some calico-printers of Manchester. The designing of calicoes can hardly be called art, even if the department of design had fallen to Holman Hunt's lot, and we have no evidence that it did; but he started to be an artist, nevertheless, there in the print shop. He found in his new place another clerk who cared for art, and this sympathy encouraged him to fix his mind upon painting more than ever. He used to draw such natural flies upon the windowpanes that his employer tried one day to "shoo away a whole colony of flies that seemed miraculously to have settled." This gave the clerks much amusement and also attracted attention to Holman Hunt's genius.

His very small salary was spent, not on his support, but in lessons from a portrait painter of the city. His parents did not like this, but they could not help themselves, and thus this greatest of the Pre-Raphaelites began his work.

Exercise 112
The Title Deed
From *The Life of Jesus Christ for the Young* by Richard Newton

Suppose that we were living in England and that we were well acquainted with Victoria—that good and gracious queen of that great kingdom. And suppose that it should please the queen to make us a present of one of the fine old castles of England with all the lands and property belonging to it. In giving us this castle, or as the lawyers say, in "conveying it to us," the queen would order a title deed to be made out. This deed would be necessary, because if any one else should claim that the castle belonged to him, we could then open the deed and show that the queen had really given it to us. A title deed, like this of which we are now speaking, is generally written on a sheet of parchment. In this deed would be found the name of the castle with a full description of it and all the property belonging to it. It would be stated here how many acres of land were connected with it; and then it would be written down that the queen had given it to us, and that it was to belong to us and to our children, or heirs, forever. But after all this had been written out, the deed would be good for nothing unless something more were done to it. It would be necessary for the queen to sign her own name to the deed—Victoria Regina—and then put the royal seal upon it. The property described in it could never become ours unless the queen's signature and seal were added to it.

The Rich Treasure
From *The Adventures of Tom Sawyer* by Mark Twain

The adventure of the day mightily tormented Tom's dreams that night. Four times he had his hands on that rich treasure, and four times it wasted to nothingness in his fingers as sleep forsook him and wakefulness brought back the hard reality of his misfortune. As he lay in the early morning recalling the incidents of his great adventure, he noticed that they seemed curiously subdued and far away—somewhat as if they had happened in another world or in a time long gone by. Then it occurred to him that the great adventure itself must be a dream! There was one very strong argument in favor of this idea: namely, that the quantity of coin he had seen was too vast to be real. He had never seen as much as fifty dollars in one mass before, and he was like all boys of his age and station in life, in that he imagined that all references to "hundreds" and "thousands" were mere fanciful forms of speech, and that no such sums really existed in the world. He never had supposed for a moment that so large a sum as a hundred dollars was to be found in actual money in any one's possession. If his notions of hidden treasure had been analyzed, they would have been found to consist of a handful of real dimes and a bushel of vague, splendid, ungraspable dollars.

Common Sense
By James Thomas Fields

She came among the gathering crowd,
A maiden fair, without pretense,
And when they asked her humble name,
She whispered mildly, "Common Sense."

Her modest garb drew every eye,
Her ample cloak, her shoes of leather;
And, when they sneered, she simply said,
"I dress according to the weather."

They argued long, and reasoned loud,
In dubious Hindu phrase mysterious,
While she, poor child, could not divine
Why girls so young should be so serious.

They knew the length of Plato's beard,
And how the scholars wrote in Saturn;
She studied authors not so deep,
And took the Bible for her pattern.

And so she said, "Excuse me, friends,
I find all have their proper places,
And Common Sense should stay at home
With cheerful hearts and smiling faces."

Exercise 115
The Lion's Voice
From *Wonders of the Tropics* by Henry Davenport Northrop

One of the most striking things connected with the lion is his voice, which is extremely grand and peculiarly striking. It consists at times of a low, deep moaning repeated five or six times, ending in faintly audible sighs; at other times he startles the forest with loud deep-toned, solemn roars repeated five or six times in quick succession, each increasing in loudness to the third or fourth, when his voice dies away in five or six low, muffled sounds, very much resembling distant thunder.

At times, and not infrequently, a troop may be heard roaring in concert, one assuming the lead and two, three, or four more regularly taking up their parts, like persons singing a catch. Like Scottish stags, they roar loudest in cold, frosty nights; but on no occasions are their voices to be heard in such perfection, or so intensely powerful, as when two or three strange troops of lions approach a fountain to drink at the same time. When this occurs, every member of each troop sounds a bold roar of defiance at the opposite parties; and when one roars, all roar together, and each seems to vie with his comrades in the intensity and power of his voice.

Exercise 116
The Babies' Names
From *The Life of Jesus Christ for the Young* by Richard Newton

When an infant is born in a family, it is generally the occasion of great interest. Many questions have to be asked and answered in connection with the little stranger. Not by any means the least interesting of these is the question What shall we call the baby? What shall its name be? Sometimes it takes a long while to answer this question. We call the little darling "baby," and that seems name enough at first.

I had a dear, good minister from Ireland staying at my house not long ago. We remember him and his visit with great delight. He had a large family of nine children. One day when we were sitting round the dinner table, I asked him what were the names of his children. In a moment he began with the oldest and repeated their names, one after another, till he had given the seventh name. Then he stopped to think. Presently he said, "Sure and I've forgotten the names of the two youngest; and the reason is we never use their names. We always call them big baby and little baby; and that's all we think of." The next day he remembered the names and gave them to us.

Exercise 117
A Night in Prison
From *The Life of Jesus Christ for the Young* by Richard Newton

One of the celebrated kings of England was Henry the Eighth, the father of the queens Elizabeth and Mary. The story is told of him that he used to disguise himself so that no one would know who he was. Then he would go about to different places in London, so that he might see what was going on in a way that he could not do if he should go there openly known as the king. On one of those occasions he got into some trouble and was taken up by the police. They had no idea that their prisoner was the king or else they would have released him in a moment. But he would not tell them who he was. And so the policemen put him in the common prison, and locked up there he had to spend the night. It was a cold, dark place, very different from his comfortable palace, and the unknown king suffered a good deal during that long dreary night.

The next morning they let him go, and he went off. On getting back to his palace, one of the first things he did was to send a sum of money to the keeper of the prison where he had spent the night. This money was to be used in furnishing fire and lights for the benefit of those who might have to be locked up in that prison all night.

Dependent on God
From *The Life and Diary of David Brainerd* by Jonathan Edwards, ed.

Had a considerable sense of my helplessness and inability; saw that I must be dependent on God for all I want, and especially when I went to the place of public worship. I found I could not speak a word for God without His special help and assistance. I went into the assembly trembling, as I frequently do, under a sense of my insufficiency to do anything in the cause of God as I ought to do. But it pleased God to afford me much assistance, and there seemed to be a considerable effect on the hearers. In the evening I felt a disposition to praise God for His goodness to me, that He had enabled me in some measure to be faithful. My soul rejoiced to think that I had thus performed the work of one day more and was one day nearer my eternal and, I trust, my Heavenly home. Oh, that I might be "faithful to the death, fulfilling as an hireling my day," till the shades of the evening of life shall free my soul from the toils of the day!

The Angel in the Stone

From *The Life of Jesus Christ for the Young* by Richard Newton

Many years ago there was a celebrated artist who lived in Italy, whose name was Michelangelo. He was a great painter and a great sculptor, or a worker in marble. He loved to see beautiful figures chiseled out of marble, and he had great power and skill in chiseling out such figures. One day, as he was walking with some friends through the city of Florence, he saw a block of marble lying neglected in a yard, half covered with dust and rubbish. He stopped to examine that block of marble. That day happened to be a great holiday in Florence, and the artist had his best suit of clothes on; but not caring for this, he threw off his coat and went to work to clear away the rubbish from that marble.

His friends were surprised. They said to him, "Come on, let's go. What's the use of wasting your time on that good-for-nothing lump of stone?"

"Oh, there's an angel in this stone," said he, "and I must get it out."

He bought that block, had it removed to his studio, and then went to work with his mallet and his chisel, and never rested till out of that rough, unshapen mass of stone he made a beautiful marble angel.

Exercise 120
Learning Outdoors
From *The Story of My Life* by Helen Keller

We read and studied out of doors, preferring the sunlit woods to the house. All my early lessons have in them the breath of the woods—the fine, resinous odor of pine needles blended with the perfume of wild grapes. Seated in the gracious shade of a wild tulip tree, I learned to think that everything has a lesson and a suggestion. "The loveliness of things taught me all their use." Indeed, everything that could hum or buzz or sing or bloom had a part in my education—noisy-throated frogs; katydids and crickets held in my hand until forgetting their embarrassment, they trilled their reedy note; little downy chickens and wildflowers; the dogwood blossoms, meadow-violets, and budding fruit trees. I felt the bursting cotton-bolls and fingered their soft fiber and fuzzy seeds; I felt the low soughing of the wind through the cornstalks, the silky rustling of the long leaves, and the indignant snort of my pony as we caught him in the pasture and put the bit in his mouth—ah me! how well I remember the spicy, clovery smell of his breath!

Native Rabbit

From *Around the World in Eighty Days* by Jules Verne

Having transacted his business at the passport office, Phileas Fogg repaired quietly to the railway station, where he ordered dinner. Among the dishes served up to him, the landlord especially recommended a certain giblet of "native rabbit," on which he prided himself.

Mr. Fogg accordingly tasted the dish, but despite its spiced sauce, found it far from palatable. He rang for the landlord, and on his appearance, said, fixing his clear eyes upon him, "Is this rabbit, sir?"

"Yes, my lord," the rogue boldly replied, "rabbit from the jungles."

"And this rabbit did not mew when he was killed?"

"Mew, my lord! What, a rabbit mew! I swear to you—"

"Be so good, landlord, as not to swear, but remember this: cats were formerly considered, in India, as sacred animals. That was a good time."

"For the cats, my lord?"

"Perhaps for the travelers as well!"

Exercise 122
Athletic Sports
From *Jo's Boys* by Louisa May Alcott

Athletic sports were in high favor at Plumfield; and the river where the old punt used to wabble about with a cargo of small boys, or echo to the shrill screams of little girls trying to get lilies, now was alive with boats of all kinds, from the slender wherry to the trim pleasure-craft, gay with cushions, awnings, and fluttering pennons. Everyone rowed, and the girls as well as the youths had their races and developed their muscles in the most scientific manner. The large, level meadow near the old willow was now the college playground, and here baseball battles raged with fury, varied by football, leaping, and kindred sports fitted to split the fingers, break the ribs, and strain the backs of the too ambitious participants. The gentler pastimes of the damsels were at a safe distance from this Champ de Mars; croquet mallets clicked under the elms that fringed the field; rackets rose and fell energetically in several tennis courts; and gates of different heights were handy to practice the graceful bound by which every girl expected to save her life some day when the mad bull, which was always coming but never seemed to arrive, should be bellowing at her heels.

An Old Woman of the Roads
By Padraic Colum

O, to have a little house!
To own the hearth and stool and all!
The heaped up sods upon the fire,
The pile of turf against the wall!

To have a clock with weights and chains
And pendulum swinging up and down!
A dresser filled with shining delph,
Speckled and white and blue and brown!

I could be busy all the day
Clearing and sweeping hearth and floor,
And fixing on their shelf again
My white and blue and speckled store!

I could be quiet there at night
Beside the fire and by myself,
Sure of a bed and loath to leave
The ticking clock and the shining delph!

Och! but I'm weary of mist and dark,
And roads where there's never a house nor bush,
And tired I am of bog and road,
And the crying wind and the lonesome hush!

And I am praying to God on high,
And I am praying Him night and day,
For a little house—a house of my own—
Out of the wind's and the rain's way.

Exercise 124
Winter Near the Wild Wood

From The Wind in the Willows by Kenneth Grahame

It was a cold still afternoon with a hard steely sky overhead when he slipped out of the warm parlor into the open air. The country lay bare and entirely leafless around him, and he thought that he had never seen so far and so intimately into the insides of things as on that winter day when Nature was deep in her annual slumber and seemed to have kicked the clothes off. Copses, dells, quarries, and all hidden places, which had been mysterious mines for exploration in leafy summer, now exposed themselves and their secrets pathetically and seemed to ask him to overlook their shabby poverty for a while till they could riot in rich masquerade as before and trick and entice him with the old deceptions. It was pitiful in a way, and yet cheering—even exhilarating. He was glad that he liked the country undecorated, hard, and stripped of its finery. He had got down to the bare bones of it, and they were fine and strong and simple. He did not want the warm clover and the play of seeding grasses; the screens of quickset, the billowy drapery of beech and elm seemed best away; and with great cheerfulness of spirit he pushed on towards the Wild Wood, which lay before him low and threatening like a black reef in some still southern sea.

Pinocchio, spurred on by the hope of finding his father and of being in time to save him, swam all night long.

And what a horrible night it was! It poured rain, it hailed, it thundered, and the lightning was so bright that it turned the night into day.

At dawn he saw, not far away from him, a long stretch of sand. It was an island in the middle of the sea.

Pinocchio tried his best to get there, but he couldn't. The waves played with him and tossed him about as if he were a twig or a bit of straw. At last, and luckily for him, a tremendous wave tossed him to the very spot where he wanted to be. The blow from the wave was so strong that as he fell to the ground, his joints cracked and almost broke. But nothing daunted, he jumped to his feet and cried, "Once more I have escaped with my life!"

Little by little the sky cleared. The sun came out in full splendor, and the sea became as calm as a lake.

Then the Marionette took off his clothes and laid them on the sand to dry. He looked over the waters to see whether he might catch sight of a boat with a little man in it. He searched and he searched, but he saw nothing except sea and sky and far away a few sails, so small that they might have been birds.

After Ten Years
From *The Swiss Family Robinson* by Johann Wyss

"We spend our years as a tale that is told," said King David. These words recurred to me again and again as I reviewed ten years, of which the story lay chronicled in the pages of my journal.

Year followed year; chapter succeeded chapter; steadily, imperceptibly, time was passing away.

The shade of sadness cast on my mind by retrospect of this kind was dispelled by thoughts full of gratitude to God for the welfare and happiness of my beloved family during so long a period. I had cause especially to rejoice in seeing our sons advance to manhood, strengthened by early training for lives of usefulness and activity wherever their lot might fall.

And my great wish is that young people who read this record of our lives and adventures, should learn from it how admirably suited is the peaceful, industrious, and pious life of a cheerful and united family to the formation of strong, pure, and manly character.

None take a better place in the great national family, none are happier or more beloved than those who go forth from such homes to fulfill new duties and to gather fresh interests around them.

Exercise 127
The Officer Helps
From *The Life of Jesus Christ for the Young* by Richard Newton

During the war of the American Revolution, the commander of a little squad of soldiers was superintending their operations as they were trying to raise a heavy piece of timber to the top of some military works, which they were engaged in repairing. It was hard work to get the timber up, and so the commander, who was a proud man and thought himself of great importance, kept calling out to them from time to time, "Push away, boys! There she goes! Heave ho!"

While this was going on, an officer on horseback, but not in military dress, rode by. He asked the commander why he did not take hold and give the men a little help. He looked at the stranger in great astonishment and then, with all the pride of an emperor, said, "Sir, I'd have you know that I am a corporal!"

"You are, are you?" replied the officer. "I was not aware of that." Then taking off his hat and making a low bow, he said, "I ask your pardon, Mr. Corporal."

After this he got off his horse, and throwing aside his coat, he took hold and helped the men at their work till they got the timber into its place. By this time the perspiration stood in drops upon his forehead. He took out his handkerchief and wiped his brow.

Then turning to the commander, he said, "Mr. Corporal, when you have another such job on hand and have not men enough to do it, send for your Commander-in-chief, and I will come and help you again."

God Does All Things Well

From *The Life of Jesus Christ for the Young* by Richard Newton

We are not told, and therefore we do not know, how many different kinds of birds and beasts and insects were taken into the ark with Noah. But God knew just how many of them there would be when he gave directions to Noah how large he was to make the ark. He never makes a mistake in doing anything.

You know we have a number of oceans on our earth. There is the Atlantic Ocean and the Pacific Ocean and the Indian Ocean and so on. And when God made these oceans he knew exactly how much water was to be put into each of them, for the Bible tells us that "He measured the waters in the hollow of his hand" (Isaiah 40:12). And so he knew how large to make the basin, or bed, which was to hold the water of each of these oceans. And in every case he has made it of the proper size.

And God is quite as careful in making little things as he is in making big things. Here is a baby; look now at the baby's eyes. Each of them is a little ball—a wonderful ball, indeed—not quite round, but rather longer one way than it is the other. And each eye has a little hole, or socket, as it is called, made for it in the bony part of the baby's head. God has made millions on millions of eyes. And each of these has had a socket exactly fitted for it. The socket for each of your eyes and each of my eyes just fits it. It is neither too large nor too small. God does all things well.

Exercise 129
The Banquet
From *The Reluctant Dragon* by Kenneth Grahame

Banquets are always pleasant things, consisting mostly, as they do, of eating and drinking; but the specially nice thing about a banquet is that it comes when something's over and there's nothing more to worry about and tomorrow seems a long way off. St. George was happy because there had been a fight and he hadn't had to kill anybody; for he didn't really like killing, though he generally had to do it. The dragon was happy because there had been a fight, and so far from being hurt in it, he had won popularity and a sure footing in society. The Boy was happy because there had been a fight, and in spite of it all, his two friends were on the best of terms. And all the others were happy because there had been a fight, and—well, they didn't require any other reasons for their happiness. The dragon exerted himself to say the right thing to everybody and proved the life and soul of the evening; while the Saint and the Boy, as they looked on, felt that they were only assisting at a feast of which the honor and the glory were entirely the dragon's. But they didn't mind that, being good fellows, and the dragon was not in the least proud or forgetful. On the contrary, every ten minutes or so he leaned over towards the Boy and said impressively: "Look here! You will see me home afterwards, won't you?" And the Boy always nodded, though he had promised his mother not to be out late.

Flamingoes
From *Wonders of the Tropics* by Henry Davenport Northrop

Presently a flash of red appeared in the blue sky, and looking up, we saw what might be described as a great fiery triangle in the air, sweeping down towards us. On it came, greatly diminishing its rate, and we then saw that it was composed of flamingoes. They hovered for a moment, then flew round and round, following one another, and gradually approached the marsh, on which they alighted. Immediately they arranged themselves as we had before seen them, in long lines, when several marched off on either side to act as sentinels while the rest commenced fishing. We could see them arching their necks and digging their long bills into the ground while they stirred up the mud with their webbed feet in order to procure the water-insects on which they subsist. They, however, were not the only visitors to the river. The tide was low, and on every mud-bank or exposed spot, countless numbers of birds were collected—numerous kinds of gulls, herons, and long-legged cranes—besides which, on the trees were perched thousands of white birds, looking at a distance like shining white flowers. Vast flocks of huge pelicans were swimming along the stream, dipping their enormous bills into the water and each time bringing up a fish. They have enormous pouches, capable of containing many pounds of their finny prey.

Exercise 131
Benjamin Franklin and Electricity
From *Swinton's Advanced Fourth Reader*

In the year 1748 Franklin was forty-two years of age. He had been in business twenty years and had acquired a modest fortune. He now resolved to abandon business and devote himself to what he loved best of all: the pursuit of science.

Franklin had already become deeply interested in electricity, a subject which now for the first time began to attract the attention of learned men. He now devoted himself wholly to electrical experiments. Out of these experiments grew the most interesting of his discoveries, namely, the identity of electricity and lightning.

He found that lightning and the electric fluid agreed in all the particulars in which they had been compared. But there was one particular in which they had not been compared. "The electric fluid," said Franklin, "is attracted by points. We do not know whether this property is in lightning. Let the experiment be tried."

Franklin proposed to use in his experiment a sharp-pointed iron rod rising from the top of some high tower. But Philadelphia at this time contained no such tower.

One day—it was in the year of 1752—he happened to observe a boy flying a kite. It instantly flashed across his mind that here was the best possible means of reaching the clouds. This leads us to the story of how he flew his immortal kite.

Exercise 132
Robert Bruce and the Spider
By Eliza Cook

Now, just at that moment, a spider dropped,
With its silken cobweb clew;
And the King, in the midst of his thinking, stopped
To see what the spider would do.

It was a long way up to the raftered dome,
And it hung by a rope so fine,
That how it would get to its cobweb home
King Bruce could not divine.

It soon began to cling and crawl
Straight up with strong endeavor;
But down it came with a slipping sprawl,
As near to the ground as ever.

Up, up, it ran, nor a second did stay
To make the least complaint,
Till it fell still lower; and there it lay,
A little dizzy and faint.

Its head grew steady,—again it went,
And climbed a half yard higher;
It was a delicate thread it had to tread,
And a road where its feet would tire.

Again it fell—and swung below;
But up it quickly mounted,
Till, up and down, now fast, now slow,
Nine brave attempts were counted.

"Sure," said the King, "that foolish thing
Will strive no more to climb,
When it toils so hard to reach and cling,
And tumbles every time."

(continued on next page)

But up the insect went once more;
Ah me! It is an anxious minute;
He's only a foot from his cobweb door—
O, say! Will he lose or win it?

Steadily—steadily—inch by inch,
Higher and higher he got,
And a bold little run, at the very last pinch,
Put him into the wished-for spot.

"Bravo! Bravo!" the King cried out
"All honor to those who try!
The spider up there defied despair;
He conquered, and why should not I?"

Thus Bruce of Scotland braced his mind:
And gossips tell the tale,
That he tried once more, as he tried before,
And that time did not fail.

Working for Father
From *Pinocchio* by Carlo Collodi

From that day on, for more than five months, Pinocchio got up every morning just as dawn was breaking and went to the farm to draw water. And every day he was given a glass of warm milk for his poor old father, who grew stronger and better day by day. But he was not satisfied with this. He learned to make baskets of reeds and sold them. With the money he received, he and his father were able to keep from starving.

Among other things, he built a rolling chair, strong and comfortable, to take his old father out for an airing on bright, sunny days.

In the evening the Marionette studied by lamplight. With some of the money he had earned, he bought himself a secondhand volume that had a few pages missing, and with that he learned to read in a very short time. As far as writing was concerned, he used a long stick at one end of which he had whittled a long, fine point. Ink he had none, so he used the juice of blackberries or cherries.

Little by little his diligence was rewarded. He succeeded not only in his studies but also in his work, and a day came when he put enough money together to keep his old father comfortable and happy. Besides this, he was able to save the great amount of fifty pennies. With it he wanted to buy himself a new suit.

Exercise 134
Dorothy Prepares to Travel
From *The Wizard of Oz* by L. Frank Baum

When Dorothy was left alone, she began to feel hungry. So she went to the cupboard and cut herself some bread, which she spread with butter. She gave some to Toto, and taking a pail from the shelf, she carried it down to the little brook and filled it with clear, sparkling water. Toto ran over to the trees and began to bark at the birds sitting there. Dorothy went to get him and saw such delicious fruit hanging from the branches that she gathered some of it, finding it just what she wanted to help out her breakfast.

Then she went back to the house, and having helped herself and Toto to a good drink of the cool, clear water, she set about making ready for the journey to the City of Emeralds.

Dorothy had only one other dress, but that happened to be clean and was hanging on a peg beside her bed. It was gingham, with checks of white and blue; and although the blue was somewhat faded with many washings, it was still a pretty frock. The girl washed herself carefully, dressed herself in the clean gingham, and tied her pink sunbonnet on her head. She took a little basket and filled it with bread from the cupboard, laying a white cloth over the top. Then she looked down at her feet and noticed how old and worn her shoes were.

"They surely will never do for a long journey, Toto," she said. And Toto looked up into her face with his little black eyes and wagged his tail to show he knew what she meant.

Exercise 135
Straight Paths
From *The Life of Jesus Christ for the Young* by Richard Newton

A light snow had fallen in a certain village, and some of the village boys met to make the best use they could of the new fallen snow. It was too dry for snow-balling and was not deep enough for coasting; so they thought they would improve the occasion by playing at making tracks in the snow.

There was a large meadow nearby with a grand old oak tree standing in the center of it. The boys gathered round the tree and stood on opposite sides, each one with his back against the tree. At a given signal they were to start and walk to the fence opposite to each of them, and then return to the tree and see which had made the straightest track.

The signal was given. They started. They reached the fence and returned to the tree.

"Now, boys, who has made the straightest track?" said one of the boys, named James Allison.

"Harry Armstrong's is the only one that is straight at all," said Thomas Sanders.

"I don't see how we all contrived to go so crooked when the meadow is so smooth and there is nothing to turn us out of the way," said one of the boys.

And then looking to their successful companion, they said, "Tell us, Harry, how you managed to make so straight a track."

Now mark what Harry said: "I fixed my eye on yonder tall pine tree on the other side of the fence towards which I was to walk and never looked away from it till I reached the fence."

The Gettysburg Address
By Abraham Lincoln

Four score and seven years ago our fathers brought forth on this continent a new nation, conceived in liberty and dedicated to the proposition that all men are created equal.

Now we are engaged in a great civil war, testing whether that nation, or any nation so conceived and so dedicated, can long endure. We are met on a great battlefield of that war. We have come to dedicate a portion of that field as a final resting place for those who here gave their lives that that nation might live. It is altogether fitting and proper that we should do this.

But in a larger sense, we cannot dedicate, we cannot consecrate, we cannot hallow this ground. The brave men, living and dead, who struggled here have consecrated it far above our poor power to add or detract. The world will little note nor long remember what we say here, but it can never forget what they did here. It is for us, the living, rather, to be dedicated here to the unfinished work which they who fought here have thus far so nobly advanced. It is rather for us to be here dedicated to the great task remaining before us: that from these honored dead we take increased devotion to that cause for which they gave the last full measure of devotion; that we here highly resolve that these dead shall not have died in vain; that this nation, under God, shall have a new birth of freedom; and that government of the people, by the people, for the people shall not perish from the earth.

Exercise 137
Escape
From *Fifty Famous People* by James Baldwin

For three days he lay in his strange prison. He grew weak from hunger and thirst. He expected to die from starvation.

Suddenly he was startled by a noise close by him. Something was moving among the rocks at the bottom of the chasm. He watched quietly and soon saw a large fox coming towards him.

He lay quite still till the animal was very near. Then he sprang up quickly and seized it by the tail.

The frightened fox scampered away as fast as it could; and Aristomenes followed, clinging to its tail. It ran into a narrow cleft which he had not seen before and then through a long, dark passage which was barely large enough for a man's body.

Aristomenes held on. At last he saw a ray of light far ahead of him. It was the sunlight streaming in at the entrance to the passage. But soon the way became too narrow for his body to pass through. What should he do? He let go of the fox, and it ran out. Then with great labor he began to widen the passageway. Here the rocks were smaller, and he soon loosened them enough to allow him to squeeze through. In a short time he was free and in the open air.

Some days after this the Spartans heard strange news: "Aristomenes is again at the head of the Greek army." They could not believe it.

First Composition

From *Fifty Famous People* by James Baldwin

The next day every pupil except one had written a composition.

"Henry Longfellow," said the teacher, "why have you not written?"

"Because I don't know how," answered Henry. He was only a child.

"Well," said the teacher, "you can write words, can you not?"

"Yes, sir," said the boy.

"After you have written three or four words, you can put them together, can you not?"

"Yes, sir; I think so."

"Well, then," said the teacher, "you may take your slate and go out behind the schoolhouse for half an hour. Think of something to write about and write the word on your slate. Then try to tell what it is, what it is like, what it is good for, and what is done with it. That is the way to write a composition."

Henry took his slate and went out. Just behind the schoolhouse was Mr. Finney's barn. Quite close to the barn was a garden. And in the garden, Henry saw a turnip.

"Well, I know what that is," he said to himself; and he wrote the word "turnip" on his slate. Then he tried to tell what it was like, what it was good for, and what was done with it.

Before the half hour was ended he had written a very neat composition on his slate. He then went into the house and waited while the teacher read it.

The teacher was surprised and pleased. He said, "Henry Longfellow, you have done very well. Today you may stand up before the school and read what you have written about the turnip."

How the Leaves Came Down
By Susan Coolidge

"I'll tell you how the leaves came down,"
The great tree to his children said,
"You're getting sleepy, Yellow and Brown,
Yes, very sleepy, little Red.
It is quite time to go to bed."

"Ah!" begged each silly, pouting leaf,
"Let us a little longer stay;
Dear Father Tree, behold our grief;
It is such a very pleasant day
We do not want to go away."

So, for just one more merry day
To the great tree the leaflets clung,
Frolicked and danced, and had their way,
Upon the autumn breezes swung,
Whispering all their sports among,—

"Perhaps the great tree will forget,
And let us stay until the spring,
If we all beg, and coax, and fret."
But the great tree did no such thing;
He smiled to hear their whispering.

"Come, children, all to bed," he cried;
And ere the leaves could urge their prayer,
He shook his head, and far and wide,
Fluttering and rustling everywhere,
Down sped the leaflets through the air.

(continued on next page)

I saw them; on the ground they lay,
Golden and red, a huddled swarm,
Waiting till one from far away,
White bedclothes heaped upon her arm,
Should come to wrap them safe and warm.

The great bare tree looked down and smiled,
"Good-night, dear little leaves," he said.
And from below each sleepy child
Replied, "Good-night," and murmured,
"It is so nice to go to bed!"

1 Corinthians 13

Though I speak with the tongues of men and of angels,

and have not charity,

I am become as sounding brass, or a tinkling cymbal.

And though I have the gift of prophecy,

and understand all mysteries, and all knowledge;

and though I have all faith, so that I could remove mountains,

and have not charity,

I am nothing.

And though I bestow all my goods to feed the poor,

and though I give my body to be burned,

and have not charity,

it profiteth me nothing.

Charity suffereth long, and is kind;

charity envieth not; charity vaunteth not itself, is not puffed up,

Doth not behave itself unseemly, seeketh not her own,

is not easily provoked, thinketh no evil;

Rejoiceth not in iniquity, but rejoiceth in the truth;

Beareth all things, believeth all things, hopeth all things, endureth all things.

Charity never faileth;

but whether there be prophecies, they shall fail;

whether there be tongues, they shall cease;

whether there be knowledge, it shall vanish away.

For we know in part, and we prophesy in part.

But when that which is perfect is come,

then that which is in part shall be done away.

When I was a child, I spake as a child,

I understood as a child, I thought as a child:

but when I became a man, I put away childish things.

For now we see through a glass, darkly; but then face to face;

now I know in part; but then shall I know even as also I am known.

And now abideth faith, hope, charity, these three;

but the greatest of these is charity.

Bibliography
Spelling Wisdom, Book Three

Adventures of Sherlock Holmes, The. Sir Arthur Conan Doyle.

Adventures of Tom Sawyer, The. Mark Twain.

Amusements in Mathematics. Henry Ernest Dudeney.

Around the World in Eighty Days. Jules Verne.

Autobiography of Benjamin Franklin, The. Benjamin Franklin.

Battle of Life, The. Charles Dickens.

Bible, The.

Black Beauty. Anna Sewell.

"Breathes There the Man." Sir Walter Scott.

Christmas Carol, A. Charles Dickens.

"Common Sense." James Thomas Fields.

"Composed Upon Westminster Bridge." William Wordsworth.

"Daffodils." William Wordsworth.

Deerslayer, The. James Fenimore Cooper.

Emma. Jane Austen.

Fifty Famous People. James Baldwin.

George Muller of Bristol. Arthur T. Pierson

Gettysburg Address, The. Abraham Lincoln.

Great Expectations. Charles Dickens.

"Home-Thoughts, from Abroad." Robert Browning.

"How Do I Love Thee?" Elizabeth Barrett Browning.

"How the Leaves Came Down." Susan Coolidge.

Hunted Down. Charles Dickens.

Jo's Boys. Louisa May Alcott.

Letters of Franz Liszt. Franz Liszt.

Life and Diary of David Brainerd, The. Jonathan Edwards, ed.

Life of Jesus Christ for the Young, The. Richard Newton.

Little Women. Louisa May Alcott.

Mansfield Park. Jane Austen.

Master Humphrey's Clock. Charles Dickens.

"Nature." Henry Wadsworth Longfellow.

Nicholas Nickleby. Charles Dickens.

Old Curiosity Shop, The. Charles Dickens.

Oliver Twist. Charles Dickens.

"Old Woman of the Roads, An." Padraic Colum.

"Peace." Henry Vaughan.

Pickwick Papers, The. Charles Dickens.

Pictures Every Child Should Know. Mary Schell Hoke Bacon.

Pilgrim's Progress, The. John Bunyan.

Pinocchio. Carlo Collodi.

Pioneers, The. James Fenimore Cooper.

Practice of Piety, The: A Puritan Devotional Manual. Lewis Bayly.

Reluctant Dragon, The. Kenneth Grahame.

"Robert Bruce and the Spider." Eliza Cook.

Robinson Crusoe. Daniel DeFoe.

Sanders' Union Fourth Reader. Charles W. Sanders.

Secret Garden, The. Frances Hodgson Burnett.

Sketch Book, The. Washington Irving.

Story of My Life, The. Helen Keller.

Swinton's Advanced Fourth Reader.

Swiss Family Robinson, The. Johann Wyss.

"Thanks for the Harvest." Laura Ingalls Wilder.

"To a Skylark." William Wordsworth.

Twenty Thousand Leagues Under the Sea. Jules Verne.

"Why Is the World So Beautiful if Not for Us?" Laura Ingalls Wilder.

Wind in the Willows, The. Kenneth Grahame.

Wizard of Oz, The. L. Frank Baum.

Wonders of the Tropics. Henry Davenport Northrop.

Wreck of the Golden Mary. Charles Dickens.

Index
Spelling Wisdom, Book Three

Blades, 124
Blasphemous, 94
Blaze, 52
Bleak, 79
Blended, 138
Blessed, 89, 105, 113
Blew, 31
Blinds, 102
Bliss, 101
Block, 62, 102, 103, 137
Blocked, 102
Blood-red, 35
Bloom, 138
Bloomgarten, 104
Blooming, 79
Blossomed, 122
Blossoms, 122, 125, 138
Blow, 143
Blowing, 74
Blue, 73, 102, 141, 148, 153
Board, 121
Boards, 99, 102
Boat, 23, 117, 143
Boats, 76, 140
Body, 53, 156, 160
Bog, 141
Boiling, 35
Boisterous, 52
Bold, 133, 151
Boldly, 139
Bole, 122
Bondage, 126
Bones, 89, 105, 142
Bony, 146
Book, 40, 71, 100
Books, 34, 118
Border, 73
Bored, 104
Born, 74, 112, 134
Borrow, 65
Both, 28, 67, 70, 78, 97, 107, 108, 110, 114, 118
Bottom, 156
Bough, 122
Boughs, 122
Bought, 65, 118, 137, 152
Bound, 140
Boundless, 35, 91
Bow, 79, 145
Bowed, 75
Bower, 126
Boy, 54, 56, 107, 147, 149, 157
Boys, 90, 128, 131, 140, 145, 154
Braced, 151
Brain, 71
Brainerd, 89, 103, 115, 136
Branch, 62
Branches, 47, 79, 153
Brass, 160
Brave, 22, 40, 119, 150, 155
Bravely, 95
Bravo, 151
Bread, 153
Breadth, 50

Break, 85, 140
Breakfast, 58, 153
Breaking, 152
Breast, 80
Breath, 50, 53, 56, 79, 138
Breathe, 91
Breathed, 115
Breathes, 91
Breeches, 78
Breeze, 101
Breezes, 158
Bribe, 93
Bridge, 81
Bridle, 105
Brief, 56
Bright, 26, 81, 143, 152
Brighter, 122
Bright-eyed, 90
Brightly, 52, 73
Brilliant, 55, 92
Bring, 27, 49, 88, 97, 126
Bringing, 148
Brings, 45
Bristol, 34, 37
Broad, 84
Broke, 143
Broken, 60, 89, 102
Bronze, 80
Brooding, 47
Broods, 92
Brook, 153
Broomstick, 100
Brot, 69
Brother, 116, 129
Brought, 64, 67, 74, 101, 108, 115, 121, 124, 126, 131, 155
Brow, 145
Brown, 110, 141, 158
Browning, 50, 122
Brows, 75
Bruce, 150, 151
Brush, 92
Brushwood, 122, 126
Budding, 138
Buds, 124
Build, 109, 110
Building, 71, 72, 102, 111
Builds, 122
Built, 85, 109, 126, 152
Bull, 140
Bunyan, 40
Buried, 53, 72, 73
Burn, 52
Burned, 82, 91, 160
Burnett, 74, 124, 127
Burning, 77
Burrow, 124
Burst, 53, 99
Bursting, 138
Bush, 117, 141
Bushel, 131
Bushels, 64
Business, 48, 69, 139, 149
Busy, 42, 71, 124, 141

But, 21, 22, 23, 28, 32, 33, 36, 40, 41, 45, 47, 48, 49, 50, 52, 53, 54, 55, 58, 59, 61, 64, 68, 69, 70, 72, 73, 74, 76, 78, 79, 82, 83, 84, 85, 86, 87, 88, 90, 93, 94, 95, 96, 97, 98, 100, 101, 102, 104, 105, 106, 107, 108, 109, 110, 112, 113, 114, 116, 117, 120, 121, 124, 126, 128, 129, 130, 133, 135, 136, 137, 139, 140, 141, 143, 145, 146, 147, 149, 150, 151, 152, 153, 155, 156, 158, 160
Butter, 107, 153
Buttercups, 122
Buttons, 71
Buy, 71, 98, 152
Buzz, 138
By, 19, 20, 21, 22, 23, 24, 25, 26, 28, 29, 30, 31, 32, 33, 34, 35, 36, 37, 38, 39, 40, 41, 42, 43, 44, 45, 46, 47, 48, 49, 50, 51, 52, 53, 54, 55, 56, 57, 58, 59, 60, 61, 62, 63, 64, 65, 66, 67, 68, 69, 70, 71, 72, 73, 74, 75, 76, 77, 78, 79, 80, 81, 82, 83, 84, 85, 87, 88, 89, 90, 91, 92, 94, 95, 96, 97, 98, 99, 100, 101, 102, 103, 104, 106, 107, 108, 112, 113, 114, 115, 116, 117, 118, 119, 120, 121, 122, 123, 124, 125, 126, 127, 129, 130, 131, 132, 133, 134, 135, 136, 137, 138, 139, 140, 141, 142, 143, 144, 145, 146, 147, 148, 149, 150, 151, 152, 153, 154, 155, 156, 157, 158

C

Cable, 121
Cables, 121
Cakes, 82
Calamity, 89
Calendar, 118
Calicoes, 129
Calico-printers, 129
Call, 56, 83, 98, 134
Called, 41, 66, 76, 118, 123, 129, 146
Calling, 145
Calm, 81, 143
Came, 47, 53, 74, 76, 77, 96, 107, 108, 117, 118, 121, 125, 126, 127, 132, 143, 148, 150, 152, 158
Can, 22, 42, 45, 50, 56, 67, 71, 85, 86, 87, 90, 91, 93, 96, 100, 103, 107, 109, 112, 113, 116, 120, 129, 155, 157
Candlelight, 50
Cannot, 110, 112, 119, 155
Canst, 70, 112
Canvas, 35, 92
Canvases, 41
Cap, 78
Capable, 68, 148
Capacity, 63
Cape, 88

Capital, 73
Capped, 99
Captain, 88
Care, 26
Cared, 129
Careful, 29, 146
Carefully, 153
Careless, 98, 122
Cares, 42, 70, 94
Cargo, 121, 140
Caring, 137
Carlo, 71, 143, 152
Carol, 25, 31
Carpenter, 78
Carriage-building, 62
Carried, 53, 55, 64, 67, 95, 97, 153
Carried-out, 63
Carries, 62
Carrying, 77, 124
Case, 46, 103, 113, 146
Cases, 51, 119
Cast, 144
Casting, 100
Castle, 76, 130
Castles, 71, 130
Catch, 59, 133, 143
Cats, 139
Caught, 128, 138
Cause, 80, 100, 107, 136, 144, 155
Caused, 123
Causes, 108
Cautious, 29
Cave, 72
Caved, 102
Cease, 160
Ceiling, 109
Celebrated, 95, 135, 137
Center, 57, 126, 154
Central, 102
Ceremony, 69
Certain, 63, 127, 139, 154
Certainly, 30, 58, 71, 72, 119
Chaffinch, 122
Chains, 141
Chair, 66, 152
Chair-carriage, 127
Chaise, 58
Champ de Mars, 140
Chance, 98
Change, 65, 93, 124
Changed, 55, 109
Changes, 68, 112
Chapter, 113, 144
Character, 19, 93, 103, 144
Characters, 51
Charity, 160
Charles, 22, 24, 25, 26, 31, 33, 35, 38, 42, 44, 45, 47, 48, 51, 52, 56, 77, 79
Charlotte, 19
Charm, 30
Charms, 79, 127

Chase, 75
Chasm, 156
Cheat, 93
Check, 65
Checks, 153
Cheeks, 74
Cheerful, 29, 52, 132, 144
Cheerfully, 103
Cheerfulness, 142
Cheerily, 47
Cheering, 49, 142
Cheese, 107
Cherishing, 90
Cherries, 152
Chickens, 138
Chiefly, 43, 118
Child, 19, 29, 41, 45, 59, 60, 86, 129, 132, 157, 159, 160
Childhood's, 50
Childish, 160
Children, 45, 59, 71, 86, 114, 115, 130, 134, 158
Children's, 122
Chill, 31
Chimneys, 102
Chisel, 137
Chiseled, 137
Chiseling, 137
Chivalry, 90
Choose, 50
Chopping, 97
Chosen, 109, 110
Christ, 29, 54, 85, 95, 113, 115, 130, 134, 135, 137, 145, 146, 154
Christlike, 29
Christlikeness, 37
Christmas, 25, 31, 66, 67
Chronicled, 144
Churchill, 32, 58
Circle, 88
Circumspect, 29
Cities, 123
City, 62, 80, 81, 129, 137, 153
Civil, 108, 155
Civilization, 120
Claim, 91, 130
Clam, 104
Clasps, 80
Class, 108
Claws, 102, 128
Clay, 111
Clean, 153
Clear, 54, 79, 137, 139, 153
Cleared, 55, 143
Clearing, 141
Cleft, 156
Clerk, 129
Clerks, 129
Clever, 71
Clew, 150
Clicked, 140
Clients, 62
Climax, 99
Climb, 32, 150

Climbed, 150
Climbing, 124
Cling, 150
Clinging, 156
Cloak, 132
Clock, 52, 83, 141
Close, 109, 156, 157
Close-fitting, 80
Cloth, 71, 153
Clothes, 78, 137, 142, 143
Clothespin, 99
Clothing, 120
Cloud, 101
Clouded, 47
Clouds, 55, 73, 77, 149
Clover, 122, 142
Clovery, 138
Clue, 67
Clung, 158
Clusters, 79
Coals, 82
Coasting, 154
Coasts, 88
Coat, 48, 71, 137, 145
Coax, 158
Coburg, 62
Cobweb, 150, 151
Cock, 114
Coffee, 62
Coin, 131
Cold, 31, 33, 71, 89, 99, 114, 133, 135, 142
Coldly, 38
Colin, 124, 127
Collected, 111, 148
College, 140
Collodi, 71, 143, 152
Colony, 129
Color, 90
Coloring, 92
Colors, 28, 92
Colum, 141
Come, 46, 68, 69, 87, 94, 105, 106, 115, 123, 125, 137, 145, 155, 158, 159, 160
Comes, 79, 85, 119, 147
Comfort, 38, 39, 120
Comfortable, 135, 152
Comfortably, 114
Comforted, 60
Comforts, 89
Comical, 99
Coming, 76, 77, 92, 109, 123, 140, 156
Command, 123
Commanded, 123
Commander, 145
Commander-in-chief, 145
Commandments, 27
Commands, 112
Commenced, 148
Commerce, 108
Common, 97, 118, 119, 132, 135
Commonly, 118

Communicative, 61
Companion, 52, 106, 154
Companions, 100, 114
Company, 69, 101
Comparatively, 37, 102
Compared, 113, 149
Compass, 105
Compassion, 56
Compelled, 65
Complaint, 150
Complete, 88
Completely, 79
Compliments, 66
Composed, 70, 72, 81, 95, 148
Composition, 51, 157
Compressed, 75
Comrades, 133
Conan, 62, 66, 67, 73, 75, 83, 102, 106
Conceived, 155
Concentered, 91
Concentrated, 75
Concerned, 152
Concert, 133
Concluded, 72
Concluding, 72
Conclusion, 27, 96
Conclusions, 84
Condition, 108
Conditions, 57, 104, 107
Condolences, 119
Conduct, 29
Confess, 103, 105
Confesses, 37
Confession, 103
Confidence, 36
Confuse, 93
Confused, 117
Congratulate, 93
Connected, 43, 108, 130, 133
Connection, 83, 134
Connects, 125
Conquered, 151
Conqueror's, 110
Consciousness, 38
Consecrate, 155
Consecrated, 155
Conseil, 88
Consider, 72, 97, 125
Considerable, 89, 118, 136
Considerably, 36
Considered, 51, 118, 126, 139
Consist, 131
Consistent, 103
Consistently, 63
Consisting, 147
Consists, 133
Consolation, 115
Constant, 52
Constantly, 76, 109, 120
Constitutes, 21
Construct, 110
Constructing, 51
Consult, 83

Contagious, 25
Contain, 40
Contained, 149
Containing, 148
Content, 93
Contests, 110
Continent, 155
Continually, 76, 125
Continue, 67
Continued, 55, 72, 118, 150, 158
Continuous, 101
Contracted, 30
Contrary, 61, 147
Contrast, 79
Contrasts, 125
Contrived, 97, 154
Control, 93
Conundrums, 62
Convenience, 68
Conventional, 24
Converse, 34
Converted, 68
Conveying, 118, 130
Cook, 82, 150
Cool, 78, 153
Coolidge, 158
Cooper, 23, 28
Cooperation, 83
Copiously, 99
Copses, 142
Corinthians, 160
Corn, 79
Corner, 62, 90, 127
Cornfields, 79
Cornstalks, 138
Corporal, 145
Correct, 39, 116
Correspond, 51
Corrupt, 94
Cost, 65, 97
Cottonbolls, 138
Couch, 66, 101
Could, 31, 36, 38, 41, 53, 58, 61, 63, 65, 67, 72, 76, 81, 84, 88, 95, 96, 97, 98, 101, 110, 113, 117, 120, 121, 122, 124, 126, 127, 128, 129, 130, 132, 135, 136, 138, 141, 142, 148, 150, 154, 156, 158, 160
Couldn't, 143
Counsel, 114
Count, 46, 50
Counted, 74, 150
Countenance, 24, 33
Countless, 148
Country, 49, 96, 112, 114, 120, 124, 126, 142
Countryman, 96
Countryside, 73
County, 80
Courage, 53, 100, 120
Courageous, 29, 100
Course, 88, 120, 123
Courteous, 29, 90
Courts, 140

Cove, 121
Cover, 82
Covered, 105, 125, 137
Cow, 107
Crab, 102
Cracked, 66, 143
Crackled, 47
Crackling, 52
Cranes, 148
Crawford, 36
Crawl, 150
Cream, 99
Created, 155
Creator, 107
Creature, 107, 123
Creatures, 26, 78, 107
Crept, 47
Crest, 100
Cricket, 52
Crickets, 138
Cried, 143, 151, 158
Crooked, 154
Crop, 64
Cropping, 65
Crops, 87
Croquet, 140
Cross, 127
Crowd, 101, 132
Crowned, 112
Cruel, 98
Cruelty, 128
Crumpled, 66
Crusoe, 53, 64, 72, 76, 78, 82, 97, 107, 117, 121, 126
Crying, 141
Cultivator, 108
Cunning, 33
Cup, 62
Cupboard, 153
Cure, 112
Curiosity, 43, 77
Curious, 61, 74
Curiously, 131
Curled, 100
Curling, 102
Curlpapers, 99
Curving, 102
Cushions, 140
Cut, 58, 121, 153
Cutting, 97, 121
Cyclist, 65
Cymbal, 160

D

Daffodils, 101
Daily, 26, 61
Dairy, 107
Damage, 93
Dame, 100
Damp, 111
Damsels, 140
Dance, 101
Danced, 101, 158
Dances, 101

Dancing, 101
Danger, 112
Dangerous, 84
Daniel, 53, 64, 72, 76, 78, 82, 97, 107, 117, 121, 126
Dare, 94
Dark, 48, 77, 135, 141, 156
Darkened, 75
Darkly, 160
Darkness, 77
Darling, 134
Daunted, 143
Davenport, 120, 133, 148
David, 89, 103, 115, 136, 144
Dawn, 143, 152
Day, 24, 32, 58, 60, 68, 71, 72, 73, 77, 89, 92, 94, 96, 99, 105, 107, 114, 116, 117, 121, 123, 124, 125, 127, 129, 131, 134, 136, 137, 140, 141, 142, 143, 149, 152, 157, 158
Day's, 50
Daybreak, 114
Days, 61, 87, 92, 118, 124, 128, 139, 152, 156
Dead, 47, 91, 155
Deaf, 59
Deal, 87, 135
Deals, 60
Dear, 46, 69, 81, 83, 90, 93, 106, 115, 119, 134, 158, 159
Death, 29, 50, 90, 97, 119, 136
Decaying, 77
December, 46, 119
Deceptions, 142
Decided, 96
Declared, 124
Decline, 108
Dedicate, 155
Dedicated, 155
Deduce, 67
Deed, 130
Deeds, 28
Deep, 53, 81, 102, 119, 125, 132, 133, 142, 154
Deepest, 38
Deeply, 149
Deeptoned, 133
Deerslayer, 28
Deference, 90
Defiance, 133
Defied, 151
Defoe, 53, 64, 72, 76, 78, 82, 97, 107, 117, 121, 126
Degree, 51, 117
Degrees, 19
Delay, 67
Delicacy, 62
Delicate, 92, 150
Delicious, 153
Delight, 134
Delightedly, 59
Delightful, 74, 92, 127
Deliverance, 105
Dells, 142

Delph, 141
Demand, 118
Departing, 77
Department, 129
Dependent, 29, 136
Depot, 62
Depth, 50
Descend, 112
Describe, 108
Described, 130, 148
Description, 116, 130
Deserted, 38, 88
Desertions, 115
Deserves, 71
Design, 76, 129
Designing, 129
Desires, 94
Desk, 48
Desolation, 47
Despair, 151
Despise, 70
Despite, 91, 139
Destiny, 67
Destroying, 95
Destruction, 107
Details, 41
Determined, 83, 104
Detract, 155
Developed, 140
Devote, 63, 149
Devoted, 29, 80, 149
Devoting, 51
Devotion, 155
Dew, 122
Dewdrops, 122
Dewy, 70
Diamond, 71
Diary, 89, 103, 115, 136
Dickens, 22, 24, 25, 26, 31, 33, 35, 38, 42, 45, 47, 48, 51, 52, 56, 77, 79
Dickon, 124, 127
Dictates, 107
Did, 36, 58, 61, 65, 67, 71, 81, 84, 92, 95, 107, 112, 121, 125, 127, 129, 135, 139, 142, 145, 150, 151, 155, 158
Didn't, 124, 147
Die, 112, 123, 156
Died, 52, 116, 155
Dies, 133
Differed, 36
Different, 28, 49, 57, 135, 140, 146
Difficult, 54, 68, 118
Difficulties, 84, 120
Difficulty, 116
Digging, 74, 148
Dilate, 75
Diligence, 152
Dim, 56
Dimes, 131
Diminishing, 148
Dine, 69

Dinner, 58, 67, 69, 134, 139
Dip, 121
Dipping, 148
Directions, 146
Directly, 128
Dirt, 49
Disagree, 86
Disappeared, 65, 79
Disappoint, 69
Disappointment, 84, 87
Discern, 58
Discourage, 93
Discouraging, 32
Discoveries, 149
Discovery, 76
Discretion, 83
Disdain, 40
Disease, 25
Disguise, 135
Dish, 139
Dishes, 139
Dishonesty, 24
Dispelled, 144
Disposed, 103
Disposition, 103, 136
Dispossess, 42
Disreputable, 66
Distance, 59, 117, 126, 140, 148
Distances, 57
Distant, 77, 133
Distress, 119
Distressing, 89
Distribute, 104
Disturbed, 111
Divine, 70, 132, 150
Division, 116
Dizzy, 150
Do, 28, 40, 44, 50, 57, 65, 69, 71, 72, 87, 93, 95, 98, 103, 104, 113, 115, 127, 135, 136, 145, 146, 147, 149, 150, 153, 155, 156, 158
Doctor, 62
Does, 22, 85, 87, 146
Dog, 98, 100
Dogcart, 106
Dogwood, 138
Doing, 85, 86, 146
Dollar, 104
Dollars, 92, 93, 104, 131
Dome, 150
Domes, 81
Domestic, 100
Domiciles, 110
Don't, 24, 93, 98, 154, 157
Done, 33, 61, 62, 72, 95, 97, 103, 104, 113, 130, 157, 160
Door, 60, 94, 100, 110, 125, 151
Doors, 55, 138
Dorothy, 153
Dost, 70
Doth, 81, 160
Double, 98, 126
Doubly, 91
Doubt, 88, 106, 120

Dower, 122
Down, 24, 73, 74, 77, 82, 91, 102, 117, 121, 127, 130, 141, 142, 148, 150, 153, 158, 159
Downward, 75
Downy, 138
Doyle, 62, 66, 67, 73, 75, 83, 102, 106
Dragon, 147
Dragon's, 147
Drapery, 142
Draw, 129, 152
Drawing, 99, 128
Drawn, 75
Dream, 56, 131
Dreams, 26, 131
Dreary, 135
Dress, 132, 145, 153
Dressed, 94, 153
Dresser, 141
Dressing-gown, 66
Drew, 23, 82, 132
Drifting, 73
Drink, 133, 153
Drinking, 147
Drive, 98, 106
Driver, 106
Drooped, 100
Drop, 70
Dropped, 54, 96, 150
Drops, 77, 128, 145
Drought, 105
Drove, 98
Dry, 78, 111, 143, 154
Dubious, 132
Dudeney, 57, 65, 96, 104, 116
Due, 87
Dull, 77, 81, 97
Dullness, 84
Dumb, 125
Dungeons, 107
During, 109, 135, 144, 145
Dust, 29, 91, 115, 137
Duties, 144
Duty, 27, 76
Dwell, 40
Dying, 91

E

Each, 54, 57, 99, 102, 113, 116, 122, 124, 127, 133, 146, 148, 154, 158, 159
Eager, 39, 59
Eagerness, 55, 128
Ear, 47
Early, 92, 99, 106, 131, 138, 144
Earn, 71
Earned, 152
Earnestly, 115
Ears, 75
Earth, 26, 47, 70, 74, 77, 79, 81, 87, 92, 111, 146, 155
Earthen, 82
Earthly, 94

Earthquakes, 72
Ease, 112
Easier, 94
Easily, 160
East, 73
Easy, 51, 86
Eat, 123
Eaten, 67
Eating, 147
Ecclesiastes, 27
Echo, 140
Eddying, 35
Edgard, 69
Edge, 73, 122
Edmund, 36
Education, 138
Edwards, 23, 89, 103, 115, 136
Effect, 136
Effective, 99
Effort, 59
Efforts, 87
Eighth, 135
Eighty, 61, 139
Either, 82, 94, 104, 148
Elaborately, 127
Elderly, 48
Electric, 149
Electrical, 149
Electricity, 149
Eleven, 73
Elfish, 124
Eliza, 150
Elizabeth, 50, 135
Elm, 142
Elms, 140
Elm-tree, 122
Else, 130, 135
Elsewhere, 77
Embarrassment, 138
Embers, 77, 82
Emeralds, 153
Emma, 30, 39, 55, 58
Emma's, 58
Emperor, 145
Employer, 129
Employment, 129
Employs, 85
Empty, 40, 116, 118
Enabled, 136
Enamored, 126
Enclose, 126
Encouraged, 129
Encouraging, 22
End, 32, 64, 102, 108, 123, 124, 152
Endeavor, 150
Endeavored, 118
Ended, 157
Ending, 133
Ends, 50
Endure, 155
Endureth, 160
Enduring, 95
Energetically, 140

Energy, 73
Engaged, 95, 145, 155
Engagement, 83
England, 97, 122, 130, 135
English, 73
Enhanced, 79
Enjoyed, 115
Enjoyment, 115
Enormous, 148
Enormously, 46
Enough, 64, 71, 119, 124, 134, 145, 152, 154, 156
Enter, 94
Entered, 100, 121, 127
Entertaining, 118
Entice, 142
Entire, 54
Entirely, 142, 147
Entrance, 156
Entreaty, 31
Envieth, 160
Epistles, 113
Equal, 42, 57, 116, 155
Equaled, 92
Equally, 120
Equestrian, 80
Equidistant, 57
Ere, 158
Erect, 110
Erected, 102
Ernest, 41, 57, 65, 96, 104, 116
Errand, 58
Errands, 124
Errors, 86
Escape, 37, 156
Escaped, 143
Especially, 116, 119, 121, 136, 139, 144
Essays, 107
Essential, 48
Estate, 34
Eternal, 115, 136
Ethereal, 70
Even, 58, 67, 83, 86, 100, 107, 109, 113, 124, 129, 142, 160
Even-handed, 25
Evening, 94, 115, 128, 136, 147, 152
Event, 83
Eventful, 125
Ever, 39, 56, 74, 85, 92, 94, 100, 103, 119, 126, 127, 129, 150
Ever-ascending, 32
Ever-improving, 32
Ever-lengthening, 32
Every, 27, 32, 35, 41, 43, 50, 57, 68, 76, 79, 92, 94, 105, 107, 113, 116, 117, 121, 124, 129, 132, 133, 140, 146, 147, 148, 150, 152, 157
Everybody, 147
Everyone, 114, 140
Everything, 121, 138
Everywhere, 158
Evidence, 129

Evidences, 120
Evident, 96
Evidently, 66, 124
Evil, 27, 37, 94, 100, 104, 160
Evil-doing, 100
Exact, 39, 62
Exactly, 61, 104, 116, 117, 146
Examination, 66
Examine, 114, 137
Examined, 102
Example, 86
Exceeding, 126
Exceedingly, 117
Excel, 40
Except, 82, 119, 143, 157
Exchange, 120
Excite, 20, 44
Excuse, 132
Execution, 97
Executive, 119
Exercise, 19, 20, 21, 22, 23, 24, 25, 26, 27, 28, 29, 30, 31, 32, 33, 34, 35, 36, 37, 38, 39, 40, 41, 42, 43, 44, 45, 46, 47, 48, 49, 50, 51, 52, 53, 54, 55, 56, 57, 58, 59, 60, 61, 62, 63, 64, 65, 66, 67, 68, 69, 70, 71, 72, 73, 74, 75, 76, 77, 78, 79, 80, 81, 82, 83, 84, 85, 86, 87, 88, 89, 90, 91, 92, 93, 94, 95, 96, 97, 98, 99, 100, 101, 102, 103, 104, 105, 106, 107, 108, 109, 110, 111, 112, 113, 114, 115, 116, 117, 118, 119, 120, 121, 122, 123, 124, 125, 126, 127, 128, 129, 130, 131, 132, 133, 134, 135, 136, 137, 138, 139, 140, 141, 142, 143, 144, 145, 146, 147, 148, 149, 150, 152, 153, 154, 155, 156, 157, 158, 160
Exerted, 113, 147
Exerting, 113
Exertion, 56
Exhilarating, 73, 142
Existed, 131
Existence, 45, 56
Expanse, 35
Expect, 63, 119
Expectant, 125
Expectations, 45
Expected, 84, 121, 140, 156
Expedition, 120
Expense, 58
Expensive, 93
Experience, 119, 128
Experiment, 149
Experiments, 149
Explained, 108
Exploration, 142
Explore, 124
Explorer, 120
Exposed, 45, 89, 142, 148
Expression, 74, 128
Exquisite, 55
Exquisitely, 41
Extenuating, 37

External, 31
Extra, 99
Extreme, 128
Extremely, 133
Eye, 33, 54, 70, 76, 100, 101, 105, 132, 146, 154
Eyes, 38, 51, 75, 85, 93, 139, 146, 153

F

Face, 22, 24, 75, 99, 125, 128, 153, 160
Faces, 132
Facetious, 96
Facility, 42
Faculties, 44
Faded, 79, 153
Fail, 151, 160
Failed, 75
Faileth, 160
Fain, 121
Faint, 47, 150
Faintly, 133
Fair, 25, 81, 91, 132
Fairly, 61
Faith, 29, 50, 115, 160
Faithful, 29, 123, 136
Faithfully, 83, 84
Fall, 59, 77, 98, 108, 144
Fallen, 129, 154
Falling, 31, 49
Falsehood, 54
Familiar, 56, 109, 125
Family, 39, 93, 102, 114, 134, 144
Famous, 120, 156, 157
Fancied, 126
Fancies, 104
Fanciful, 131
Fancy, 117
Fancying, 117
Fanny, 68, 119
Far, 32, 36, 60, 76, 96, 112, 122, 131, 139, 142, 143, 147, 152, 155, 156, 158, 159
Farm, 152
Farmsteads, 73
Farther, 117
Fast, 94, 150, 156
Fate, 114, 126
Father, 71, 93, 119, 129, 135, 143, 152, 158
Father's, 39, 115
Fathers, 71, 155
Fatigued, 114, 121
Fault, 84, 103
Favor, 120, 131, 140
Fear, 27, 106, 128
Feared, 88
Feast, 147
Feather, 124
Feature, 99
Feeble, 90
Feed, 107, 160
Feeding, 110

Feel, 53, 103, 119, 153
Feeling, 50, 95, 117, 119, 127
Feet, 47, 53, 90, 110, 143, 148, 150, 153
Fell, 75, 89, 100, 116, 125, 140, 143, 150
Fellow's, 96
Fellows, 147
Felt, 43, 45, 49, 53, 81, 115, 128, 136, 138, 147
Female, 109
Females, 110
Fence, 126, 154
Fenimore, 23, 28
Ferrets, 124
Fete, 99
Few, 29, 63, 128, 143, 152
Fiber, 138
Fidelity, 21
Field, 54, 68, 122, 140, 155
Fields, 79, 81, 122, 132
Fierce, 109
Fiery, 148
Fifty, 131, 152, 156, 157
Fight, 108, 110, 147
Figures, 47, 137
Files, 112
Fill, 94
Filled, 94, 111, 118, 125, 126, 141, 153
Fills, 101
Final, 155
Find, 40, 57, 90, 95, 113, 132
Finder, 67
Finding, 143, 153
Fine, 41, 99, 122, 130, 138, 142, 150, 152
Finely, 45
Finery, 142
Finest, 85
Fingered, 138
Fingers, 90, 125, 131, 140
Finished, 46
Finney, 157
Finny, 148
Fire, 52, 77, 128, 135, 141
Firewood, 82
Firm, 29
First, 26, 34, 54, 59, 71, 78, 81, 92, 94, 96, 107, 114, 118, 122, 134, 135, 149, 157
Fish, 148
Fishing, 23, 148
Fit, 78, 121
Fits, 146
Fitted, 140, 146
Fitting, 155
Five, 57, 133, 152
Fix, 128, 129
Fixed, 127, 154
Fixing, 139, 141
Flamingoes, 148
Flash, 101, 148
Flashed, 149

Flat, 57
Flecked, 73
Fleecy, 73
Flesh, 82, 107
Fleshly, 94
Flew, 148, 149
Flies, 129
Floats, 101
Flocks, 109, 148
Flood, 70
Floods, 105
Floor, 60, 141
Florence, 137
Florida, 109
Flourish, 100
Flower, 56, 112
Flowerbeds, 127
Flowers, 79, 92, 148
Fluid, 149
Flushed, 75
Fluttering, 35, 101, 117, 140, 158
Fly, 100
Flying, 149
Fogg, 61, 139
Fogg's, 61
Foliage, 73, 92
Follow, 87, 113
Followed, 144, 156
Following, 55, 58, 96, 148
Follows, 42, 122
Fond, 60, 69, 126
Food, 43, 64, 107, 108, 123, 124
Fool, 96
Foolish, 98, 112, 150
Foot, 97, 117, 151
Football, 140
Footing, 147
Footprint, 117
Footsteps, 91
Foppery, 58
For, 22, 27, 28, 29, 33, 41, 43, 44, 46, 49, 50, 51, 54, 55, 58, 61, 63, 64, 65, 66, 69, 71, 72, 75, 76, 78, 82, 85, 86, 87, 88, 89, 90, 91, 92, 93, 94, 95, 97, 98, 99, 100, 101, 103, 104, 105, 107, 108, 109, 110, 111, 112, 113, 114, 115, 117, 118, 120, 121, 123, 125, 126, 127, 129, 130, 131, 132, 134, 135, 136, 137, 139, 141, 142, 143, 144, 145, 146, 147, 148, 149, 152, 153, 154, 155, 156, 157, 158, 160
Force, 53
Forceps, 66
Forearm, 106
Forego, 103
Forehead, 99, 145
Foreign, 91
Forest, 133
Forever, 113, 130
Forfeit, 91
Forgavest, 105
Forget, 86, 155, 158
Forgetful, 147

Forgetting, 68, 138
Forgiven, 105
Forgiveness, 103
Forgot, 65
Forgotten, 134
Form, 51, 57, 63, 113
Formation, 144
Former, 93
Formerly, 139
Forms, 131
Forsakes, 37
Forsook, 131
Forth, 94, 125, 144, 155
Fortification, 117
Fortitude, 44
Fortress, 112
Fortune, 61, 80, 149
Fortunes, 63
Forty-two, 149
Forward, 49, 53, 82, 106, 120
Fought, 155
Found, 40, 53, 65, 89, 105, 107, 111, 116, 123, 129, 130, 131, 136, 139, 149
Fountain, 74, 127, 133
Four, 57, 83, 116, 131, 133, 155, 157
Four-footed, 78
Fourteen, 113
Fourth, 44, 57, 80, 109, 110, 111, 123, 128, 133, 149
Fowls, 82
Fox, 156
Foxes, 124
Frances, 74, 124, 127
Frank, 58, 153
Franklin, 118, 149
Franz, 46, 63, 69
Freak, 58
Free, 80, 136, 156
Freedom, 155
Freely, 50, 88, 92, 120
French, 69
Frenchman, 80
Frequent, 63
Frequented, 88
Frequently, 89, 136
Fresh, 74, 79, 106, 111, 144
Freshness, 92
Fret, 158
Friend, 65, 66, 112, 119
Friendly, 29
Friends, 104, 132, 137, 147
Friendship, 46
Frightened, 156
Fringed, 140
Fro, 125
Frock, 153
Frogs, 124, 138
Frolicked, 158
From, 20, 22, 23, 24, 25, 26, 28, 29, 30, 31, 32, 33, 34, 35, 36, 37, 38, 39, 40, 41, 42, 43, 44, 45, 46, 47, 48, 49, 50, 51, 52, 53, 54, 55,

56, 57, 58, 59, 61, 62, 63, 64, 65, 66, 67, 68, 69, 71, 72, 73, 74, 75, 76, 77, 78, 79, 80, 82, 83, 84, 85, 88, 89, 90, 91, 93, 94, 95, 96, 97, 98, 99, 100, 102, 103, 104, 105, 106, 107, 109, 110, 111, 113, 114, 115, 116, 117, 118, 120, 121, 122, 123, 124, 125, 126, 127, 128, 129, 130, 131, 133, 134, 135, 136, 137, 138, 139, 140, 142, 143, 144, 145, 146, 147, 148, 149, 151, 152, 153, 154, 155, 156, 157, 159
Front, 109
Frontier, 84
Frost, 67, 92
Frosty, 47, 133
Frugality, 118
Fruit, 79, 138, 153
Fruitful, 32
Fulfill, 67, 144
Fulfilling, 136
Full, 60, 97, 116, 130, 143, 144, 155
Fully, 120
Funny, 99
Furnished, 120
Furnishing, 135
Further, 63
Fury, 35, 140
Fussed, 90
Future, 125
Fuzzy, 138

G

Gained, 54
Gaiters, 48
Gallant, 80
Gallon, 107
Gallows, 100
Garb, 132
Garden, 74, 124, 127, 157
Gardener, 54, 127
Garlands, 47
Garment, 81
Gates, 140
Gather, 144
Gathered, 77, 153, 154
Gathering, 132
Gaudy, 122
Gave, 41, 53, 65, 106, 124, 129, 134, 146, 153, 155
Gay, 101, 122, 140
Gazed, 101
Gazing, 60
General, 80
Generally, 118, 130, 134, 147
Generals, 127
Genius, 129
Gentle, 29, 56
Gentleman, 67, 96
Gentlemen, 51, 90
Gentler, 140
Gently, 60
George, 34, 37, 147

Get, 32, 112, 113, 121, 137, 140, 143, 145, 150, 153
Getting, 77, 135, 158
Gettysburg, 155
Giblet, 139
Gift, 104, 160
Gifts, 28
Gingham, 153
Girl, 140, 153
Girls, 90, 99, 132, 140
Give, 30, 69, 85, 87, 103, 104, 107, 115, 123, 145, 160
Given, 90, 103, 104, 116, 130, 134, 152, 154
Gives, 55, 85, 92, 107
Giving, 130
Glad, 39, 43, 77, 89, 105, 142
Glance, 96, 100, 101
Glancing, 51, 62
Glare, 49
Glass, 76, 152, 160
Gleamed, 77
Glee, 101
Glideth, 81
Glitter, 75
Glittering, 81
Glorious, 70, 92
Glory, 32, 77, 147
Glove, 106
Glows, 52
Go, 60, 91, 98, 104, 105, 127, 135, 137, 144, 154, 156, 157, 158, 159
Goal, 84
Goat, 107
Goat's, 107
Goats, 82
God, 27, 37, 50, 54, 81, 85, 87, 89, 94, 103, 112, 115, 136, 141, 144, 146, 155
God's, 94, 115
Godliness, 94
Godly, 105
Goes, 145
Going, 88, 100, 109, 117, 126, 127, 135, 145
Gold, 40, 71, 77
Golden, 22, 79, 101, 159
Gone, 23, 56, 58, 95, 113, 131
Good, 25, 27, 58, 63, 64, 69, 71, 82, 90, 93, 96, 98, 106, 113, 121, 130, 134, 135, 139, 147, 153, 157
Good-for-nothing, 137
Goodness, 87, 136
Goodnight, 159
Goods, 121, 160
Goose, 67
Gossips, 151
Got, 24, 65, 121, 135, 142, 145, 151, 152
Government, 155
Grace, 50
Graceful, 79, 140
Gracious, 112, 130, 138

Gradually, 55, 59, 77, 148
Grahame, 142, 147
Grains, 85
Grammar, 86
Grammatical, 86
Grand, 97, 133, 154
Grapes, 138
Grass, 124
Grasses, 92, 142
Grateful, 29
Gratefully, 90
Gratitude, 144
Gray, 73, 102, 124
Great, 30, 41, 43, 45, 53, 69, 72, 78, 85, 87, 92, 97, 98, 105, 107, 113, 120, 121, 127, 128, 130, 131, 134, 137, 142, 144, 145, 148, 152, 155, 156, 158, 159
Greatest, 51, 127, 129, 160
Greatly, 53, 148
Greed, 93
Greek, 156
Green, 73, 79, 80
Greet, 125
Greeted, 47
Greetings, 63
Grew, 120, 149, 150, 152, 156
Grief, 119, 158
Griefs, 50
Grim, 26
Grind, 97
Grindstone, 97
Ground, 54, 70, 79, 100, 110, 117, 143, 148, 150, 155, 159
Grounds, 39
Grow, 37, 94
Growing, 87, 124
Grown, 41
Grows, 112
Growth, 68
Grumbling, 87
Guess, 84
Guessed, 125
Guessing, 84
Guide, 105, 121
Guile, 105
Guilty, 103
Guises, 65
Gulls, 148
Gusts, 74

H

Habit, 51
Habits, 19, 61
Had, 23, 30, 31, 36, 39, 41, 43, 49, 55, 56, 58, 59, 61, 62, 64, 65, 66, 72, 73, 74, 75, 76, 77, 78, 82, 84, 89, 96, 97, 99, 101, 102, 104, 106, 107, 109, 110, 111, 114, 116, 117, 119, 120, 121, 123, 124, 125, 126, 127, 128, 129, 130, 131, 134, 135, 136, 137, 138, 140, 142, 144, 146, 147, 148, 149, 150, 152, 153, 154, 156, 157, 158

Hadn't, 147
Hailed, 143
Hair, 58, 78
Haircut, 58
Half, 49, 60, 106, 137, 150, 157
Half-full, 116
Hallow, 155
Hammers, 19
Hampshire, 73
Hand, 60, 66, 80, 105, 107, 121, 138, 145, 146
Handful, 131
Handily, 121
Handkerchief, 145
Hands, 45, 53, 97, 98, 124, 131
Handy, 140
Hanging, 153
Happen, 125, 126
Happened, 117, 131, 137, 149, 153
Happening, 128
Happier, 56, 144
Happiness, 21, 44, 144, 147
Happy, 104, 115, 119, 147, 152
Hard, 57, 75, 76, 78, 80, 84, 97, 118, 131, 142, 145, 150
Hard-felt, 66
Hard-fought, 95
Hardly, 129
Hardness, 123
Hark, 122
Harm, 58, 104, 121
Harmony, 62, 70
Harness, 98
Harry, 154
Hartfield, 55
Harvest, 64, 87
Has, 30, 52, 63, 67, 79, 81, 83, 87, 89, 90, 92, 93, 103, 113, 123, 138, 146, 154
Hastily, 96
Hat, 66, 67, 145
Hatchets, 97
Hated, 129
Hath, 91
Have, 21, 24, 28, 33, 38, 40, 43, 45, 46, 48, 49, 54, 56, 57, 58, 59, 62, 63, 64, 67, 69, 75, 77, 78, 79, 83, 85, 87, 89, 90, 92, 93, 94, 95, 97, 98, 103, 105, 106, 109, 110, 111, 113, 114, 115, 119, 120, 121, 123, 129, 131, 132, 134, 135, 138, 141, 142, 143, 145, 146, 148, 155, 157, 160
Having, 28, 58, 65, 76, 90, 121, 127, 139, 153
Havoc, 111
Hawser, 121
He, 23, 31, 33, 35, 36, 37, 41, 42, 47, 48, 51, 54, 56, 58, 61, 63, 65, 66, 67, 71, 73, 74, 75, 80, 81, 83, 85, 88, 89, 91, 93, 95, 96, 99, 100, 103, 104, 105, 106, 107, 108, 109, 112, 113, 114, 116, 120, 122, 123,

Ingalls, 87, 92
Ingenious, 95
Ingenuity, 120
Inhabitant, 96
Iniquity, 105, 160
Injuries, 103
Injustice, 45
Ink, 152
Inkling, 40
Innumerable, 117
Inoculate, 104
Inquire, 108
Inquiries, 96
Insect, 124, 151
Insects, 146
Insides, 142
Insignificant, 128
Instances, 103
Instant, 77
Instantly, 149
Instead, 37, 48, 49, 119
Instinct, 70
Instruct, 105
Instruction, 118
Instructions, 116
Instruments, 128
Insufficiency, 136
Intelligence, 96
Intended, 128
Intending, 58
Intensely, 133
Intensity, 133
Intent, 31
Intention, 66
Interest, 67, 134
Interested, 74, 149
Interesting, 39, 134, 149
Interests, 144
Interior, 41
Interval, 114
Intimately, 142
Intimidating, 86
Into, 23, 27, 35, 49, 54, 55, 68, 70, 74, 75, 82, 85, 88, 95, 97, 98, 99, 102, 105, 107, 114, 121, 123, 127, 129, 135, 136, 142, 143, 145, 146, 148, 151, 153, 156, 157
Introduce, 55
Invention, 44
Inviolable, 104
Invisible, 115
Involved, 116
Inward, 101
Ireland, 134
Iron, 121, 149
Ironwork, 121
Irresistibly, 25
Irving, 100
Is, 21, 24, 25, 27, 30, 34, 37, 38, 40, 42, 45, 46, 51, 52, 54, 57, 59, 60, 62, 63, 64, 65, 68, 69, 70, 78, 79, 80, 81, 83, 86, 87, 88, 90, 91, 92, 93, 95, 96, 97, 98, 100, 101, 103, 105, 106, 108, 109, 112, 118, 119, 120, 123, 125, 128, 130, 133, 134, 135, 139, 144, 146, 147, 149, 151, 154, 155, 156, 157, 158, 159, 160
Isaiah, 146
Island, 64, 72, 76, 126, 143
Isn't, 71
It, 19, 21, 22, 23, 24, 25, 27, 30, 37, 39, 40, 42, 43, 45, 48, 51, 52, 53, 54, 55, 57, 58, 59, 61, 64, 67, 68, 69, 71, 72, 73, 74, 76, 77, 79, 80, 82, 83, 84, 85, 86, 87, 88, 93, 94, 95, 96, 97, 98, 99, 100, 103, 104, 107, 108, 110, 111, 113, 114, 115, 116, 117, 118, 119, 120, 121, 123, 124, 125, 126, 127, 128, 129, 130, 131, 133, 134, 135, 136, 137, 139, 142, 143, 144, 145, 146, 147, 148, 149, 150, 151, 152, 153, 154, 155, 156, 157, 158, 159, 160
It's, 62
Italy, 46, 123, 137
Its, 31, 33, 45, 49, 52, 53, 54, 57, 67, 68, 81, 85, 92, 93, 109, 120, 123, 124, 127, 128, 134, 139, 142, 145, 148, 150, 156
Itself, 33, 123, 131, 160
Ivied, 127

J

Jacket, 106
James, 23, 28, 132, 154, 156, 157
Jane, 20, 30, 36, 39, 43, 49, 55, 58, 68
Jealous, 109
Jean, 41
Jesus, 29, 54, 85, 95, 113, 115, 130, 134, 135, 137, 145, 146, 154
Jo, 99
Jo's, 140
Joanna, 99
Job, 145
Jocund, 101
Johann, 114, 144
John, 40
Joined, 110
Joints, 143
Jonathan, 89, 103, 115, 136
Journal, 144
Journey, 32, 89, 120, 153
Journeys, 89
Joy, 32, 105
Judge, 36, 97, 123
Judgment, 27, 36, 83
Juice, 152
Jules, 61, 88, 139
July, 126
Jumped, 96, 143
Jumping, 84
Jungles, 139
Just, 29, 62, 90, 98, 111, 125, 146, 150, 152, 153, 157, 158
Justice, 123
Justify, 103

K

Katydids, 138
Keep, 27, 53, 78, 82, 85, 86, 93, 94, 98, 152
Keeper, 135
Keller, 21, 59, 84, 125, 138
Kenneth, 142, 147
Kept, 46, 76, 80, 90, 94, 105, 111, 145
Key, 34, 59, 86
Kicked, 142
Kill, 128, 147
Killed, 78, 139
Killing, 147
Kind, 29, 48, 69, 99, 119, 126, 144, 160
Kindness, 63, 89
Kindred, 70, 140
Kinds, 98, 140, 146, 148
King, 92, 104, 123, 135, 144, 150, 151
Kingdom, 115, 130
Kings, 135
Kitchen, 74
Kite, 149
Knees, 78, 89, 103
Knew, 61, 104, 116, 117, 132, 146, 153
Knotty, 97
Know, 32, 41, 46, 60, 87, 93, 106, 108, 119, 125, 129, 135, 145, 146, 149, 157, 160
Knowing, 60, 67
Knowledge, 62, 160
Known, 24, 56, 75, 104, 119, 135, 160
Knows, 57, 95, 98

L

Labor, 79, 121, 156
Laboring, 35
Labors, 114
Ladder, 126
Ladies, 51, 90
Ladle, 100
Lady, 106
Lafayette, 80
Laid, 76, 143
Lake, 23, 101, 143
Lamp, 94
Lamplight, 152
Land, 54, 80, 88, 91, 130
Landed, 121
Landlord, 139
Lands, 130
Landscape, 79
Language, 59
Languor, 125
Lapped, 128
Large, 77, 93, 97, 110, 111, 113, 121, 131, 134, 140, 146, 154, 156
Larger, 41, 155
Lashed, 35
Last, 46, 61, 74, 89, 107, 113, 114, 117, 124, 143, 151, 155, 156
Late, 114, 115, 147
Latter, 48
Laugh, 99
Laughter, 25
Laura, 87, 92
Lavish, 61
Lawn, 102, 110
Laws, 108
Lawyers, 130
Lay, 57, 89, 92, 126, 131, 142, 144, 150, 156, 159
Laying, 153
Lead, 133
Leads, 60, 149
Leaf, 122, 158
Leafless, 142
Leaflets, 158
Leafy, 142
Leagues, 88
Leaned, 147
Leans, 122
Leaping, 140
Learn, 29, 59, 71, 119, 144
Learned, 119, 138, 149, 152
Learning, 138
Least, 23, 61, 76, 85, 97, 100, 117, 126, 134, 147, 150
Leather, 132
Leave, 39, 60, 65, 70, 112, 121, 141
Leaves, 47, 92, 125, 128, 138, 158, 159
Lectured, 90
Led, 60
Left, 51, 77, 80, 106, 116, 153
Left-hand, 106
Legend, 26
Legs, 100
Length, 97, 132
Lengthen, 123
Lens, 66
Less, 31, 106, 107, 119, 120
Lesson, 138
Lessons, 129, 138
Lest, 105, 122
Lestrade, 83
Let, 27, 50, 62, 82, 93, 94, 135, 149, 156, 158
Let's, 137
Lets, 37
Letter, 43, 51
Letters, 46, 51, 63, 69
Level, 50, 51, 140
Lewis, 94
Liberal, 29
Liberty, 80, 97, 128, 155
Lichen-blotched, 102
Lie, 81, 82, 101, 115, 124
Life, 28, 29, 47, 50, 54, 56, 59, 84, 85, 87, 89, 95, 97, 103, 112, 113, 115, 116, 123, 125, 128, 129, 130, 131, 134, 135, 136, 137, 138, 140, 143, 144, 145, 146, 147, 154

Lifted, 74
Light, 47, 70, 73, 79, 85, 92, 154, 156
Lightning, 77, 143, 149
Lights, 26, 135
Like, 34, 36, 44, 46, 47, 54, 56, 62, 64, 75, 81, 84, 90, 92, 94, 98, 102, 104, 113, 117, 124, 129, 130, 131, 133, 142, 147, 148, 157
Liked, 127, 142
Likely, 30
Lilies, 140
Lincoln, 119, 155
Line, 23, 59, 62, 101
Lines, 75, 148
Lingered, 125
Lion, 133
Lion's, 133
Lions, 133
Lip-reading, 84
Lips, 59, 75
Listen, 109
Listened, 117
Liszt, 46, 63, 69
Literature, 108
Little, 19, 31, 40, 45, 46, 54, 58, 59, 60, 61, 62, 65, 72, 73, 74, 78, 80, 82, 85, 90, 99, 101, 102, 110, 115, 118, 121, 122, 126, 128, 134, 138, 140, 141, 143, 145, 146, 150, 151, 152, 153, 155, 158, 159
Live, 82, 90, 109, 155
Lived, 137
Lives, 87, 92, 123, 125, 144, 155
Living, 72, 91, 93, 130, 155
Loaded, 121
Loaf, 82
Loath, 141
Loaves, 82
Local, 96
Locked, 135
Logician, 75
London, 58, 62, 135
Loneliness, 55
Lonely, 90, 101
Lonesome, 141
Long, 34, 39, 56, 75, 88, 89, 90, 96, 105, 115, 123, 124, 126, 127, 131, 132, 134, 135, 138, 143, 144, 147, 148, 150, 152, 153, 155, 156, 160
Longed, 55
Longer, 93, 146, 158
Longfellow, 60, 157
Long-legged, 148
Long-nailed, 124
Look, 20, 33, 38, 39, 40, 41, 85, 117, 122, 124, 146, 147
Looked, 74, 96, 100, 108, 117, 124, 128, 143, 145, 147, 153, 154, 159
Looking, 24, 68, 76, 117, 127, 148, 154
Looks, 63

Loose, 78
Loosened, 156
Lord, 83, 105, 115, 139
Lose, 42, 50, 65, 127, 151
Loss, 97
Lost, 50, 67, 89, 121
Lot, 71, 129, 144
Loud, 132, 133
Loudest, 133
Loudly, 114
Loudness, 133
Louis, 41
Louisa, 90, 99, 140
Lounging, 66
Love, 50, 56, 90, 93, 112, 113
Loved, 52, 137, 149
Loveliness, 138
Lovely, 92
Lover, 128
Loving, 29, 93
Low, 34, 77, 92, 133, 138, 142, 145, 148
Lower, 123, 150
Lowering, 77
Lowest, 122
Loyal, 38
Luck, 121
Luckily, 143
Lump, 137
Lust, 75, 93
Lying, 66, 81, 94, 137

M

Machine, 65, 97
Machinery, 22
Mad, 140
Madam, 106
Made, 44, 49, 61, 76, 78, 82, 85, 95, 99, 103, 107, 110, 115, 121, 127, 130, 137, 146, 154
Magistrate, 123
Magnitude, 42
Maiden, 132
Maids, 90
Main, 28
Majesty, 81
Make, 29, 32, 33, 40, 63, 69, 71, 72, 80, 95, 96, 103, 104, 107, 118, 119, 121, 124, 130, 146, 150, 152, 154
Makes, 85, 109, 146
Making, 111, 115, 116, 124, 145, 146, 153, 154
Males, 109, 110
Mallet, 137
Mallets, 140
Man, 19, 22, 27, 36, 37, 40, 42, 44, 48, 71, 80, 91, 93, 96, 97, 103, 104, 105, 113, 116, 117, 118, 120, 143, 145, 156, 160
Man's, 73, 93, 117
Managed, 114, 154
Manchester, 129
Manger, 112

Manhood, 144
Manly, 144
Manner, 20, 61, 66, 140
Mansfield, 20, 36, 43, 49, 68, 125
Mansion, 119
Many, 19, 21, 36, 45, 63, 79, 80, 86, 89, 95, 98, 100, 104, 105, 107, 109, 110, 120, 130, 134, 137, 146, 148, 153
Marble, 137
March, 125, 127
Marched, 128, 148
Margin, 101
Mariner, 44
Marionette, 143, 152
Mark, 91, 131, 154
Marks, 56, 106
Marsh, 148
Marvel, 125
Mary, 22, 41, 127, 129, 135
Mason, 19
Masquerade, 142
Mass, 125, 131, 137
Masses, 77
Mast, 35
Master, 52, 98, 100
Master's, 100
Mate, 110
Material, 95, 111
Materials, 111
Maternal, 90
Mates, 109
Mathematics, 57, 65, 96, 104, 116
Matter, 27, 29, 57, 75, 83, 90, 93, 110
Matters, 106
Mature, 103
Matured, 46
May, 32, 40, 42, 45, 46, 60, 68, 79, 83, 86, 87, 90, 92, 94, 98, 99, 104, 113, 122, 133, 140, 157
Mayest, 105
McFarlane's, 62
Me, 46, 50, 52, 53, 62, 64, 67, 69, 71, 72, 78, 83, 89, 92, 97, 98, 101, 103, 105, 106, 107, 114, 115, 117, 118, 121, 125, 126, 128, 132, 136, 138, 144, 147, 151, 160
Meadow, 140, 154
Meadow-violets, 138
Mean, 78, 98
Meaning, 86
Means, 42, 78, 90, 97, 115, 118, 126, 134, 149
Meant, 41, 153
Measure, 87, 136, 155
Measured, 146
Meditation, 43
Meditations, 94
Meek, 29
Meet, 34, 69
Meg, 99
Meissonier, 41
Melancholy, 49, 55

Mellow, 54
Melonflower, 122
Melt, 26
Member, 133
Memory, 39, 56, 80
Men, 23, 24, 28, 29, 50, 61, 72, 75, 85, 95, 98, 145, 149, 155, 160
Menaced, 77
Mention, 56
Mentioned, 78
Merchant, 116, 129
Mercies, 89
Mercifully, 107
Mercy, 37, 87, 105, 128
Mere, 42, 131
Merely, 58, 108
Merry, 52, 158
Met, 154, 155
Mew, 139
Michelangelo, 137
Microscopic, 41
Middle, 143
Midnight, 52
Midst, 150
Might, 49, 53, 55, 63, 72, 83, 85, 93, 95, 97, 103, 114, 117, 126, 135, 136, 143, 144, 148, 155
Mightily, 131
Mighty, 53, 81, 85
Migrated, 109
Mild, 29
Mildly, 132
Miles, 58, 76
Military, 108, 145
Milk, 107, 152
Milked, 107
Milky, 101
Million, 104
Millionaire, 104
Millions, 146
Mind, 29, 30, 56, 68, 72, 75, 86, 128, 129, 144, 147, 149, 151
Minds, 79
Mine, 62, 105
Mines, 142
Minister, 134
Minstrel, 70, 91
Minute, 151
Minutes, 147
Miraculously, 129
Miscarriages, 107
Miserable, 119
Misfortune, 131
Miss, 69
Missing, 152
Mist, 141
Mistake, 119, 146
Mistaking, 117
Mixture, 48
Mizzen-yard, 121
Moan, 77
Moaning, 133
Moderation, 58
Modern, 102

Modest, 132, 149
Moist, 111
Moisture, 105
Mole, 124
Moment, 100, 102, 128, 131, 134, 135, 148, 150
Monday, 69
Money, 29, 61, 65, 71, 93, 104, 120, 131, 135, 152
Monsieur, 69
Month, 79, 126
Months, 49, 76, 125, 152
Mood, 101
Moon, 47, 114
More, 31, 36, 39, 46, 49, 54, 55, 58, 60, 61, 63, 68, 70, 72, 74, 76, 79, 81, 84, 86, 89, 93, 94, 98, 103, 104, 109, 111, 115, 116, 117, 118, 127, 128, 129, 130, 133, 136, 143, 144, 147, 150, 151, 152, 158
Morgan, 104
Morning, 55, 66, 67, 73, 76, 81, 92, 94, 97, 99, 106, 122, 124, 131, 135, 152
Mortimer's, 62
Most, 50, 63, 64, 68, 75, 103, 109, 121, 125, 127, 128, 129, 133, 140, 149
Mostly, 147
Mother, 60, 69, 90, 98, 119, 147
Mother's, 125
Motions, 51
Mound, 124
Mountains, 160
Mounted, 65, 150
Mouse, 128
Mouth, 105, 138
Move, 121
Moving, 156
Mr., 36, 48, 61, 83, 104, 127, 139, 145, 157
Much, 22, 41, 43, 48, 55, 63, 65, 66, 67, 69, 82, 86, 89, 97, 100, 103, 107, 111, 115, 116, 121, 126, 129, 131, 133, 136, 146
Mud, 106, 111, 148
Mud-bank, 148
Muffled, 133
Mule, 105
Muller, 34, 37
Multiplying, 104
Murmur, 47
Murmured, 159
Murmurs, 77
Muscles, 140
Music, 56, 70
Must, 36, 39, 59, 72, 78, 105, 106, 108, 120, 127, 131, 136, 137
Mutters, 52
My, 40, 46, 50, 52, 53, 59, 66, 69, 72, 76, 78, 82, 83, 84, 89, 91, 93, 96, 97, 98, 101, 103, 105, 106, 107, 109, 110, 111, 112, 114, 115, 117, 118, 119, 121, 122, 125, 126,

128, 134, 136, 138, 139, 141, 143, 144, 146, 154, 160
Myself, 53, 72, 82, 84, 89, 117, 121, 126, 141
Mysteries, 160
Mysterious, 61, 127, 132, 142
Mystery, 106, 127

N

Nailbrush, 63
Naked, 117
Name, 80, 91, 95, 98, 118, 130, 132, 134, 137
Named, 80, 154
Namely, 34, 131, 149
Names, 95, 134
Naming, 59
Narrow, 156
Nation, 108, 155
National, 144
Native, 91, 139
Natural, 129
Naturally, 107
Nature, 28, 55, 60, 79, 92, 107, 114, 124, 142
Nautilus, 88
Near, 66, 76, 105, 110, 111, 115, 118, 121, 140, 142, 150, 156
Nearby, 154
Nearer, 126, 136
Nearly, 51
Neat, 157
Necessary, 51, 84, 99, 120, 130
Neck, 75
Necks, 148
Ned, 88
Need, 50
Needed, 61
Needle, 85
Needles, 138
Neglected, 137
Neighbor, 65
Neighborhood, 118
Neighboring, 65
Neither, 23, 44, 82, 146
Nemo, 88
Nerve, 120
Nest, 70, 109, 110
Nests, 110, 111
Never, 22, 32, 37, 43, 44, 55, 56, 68, 70, 81, 89, 91, 97, 98, 104, 107, 110, 112, 122, 130, 131, 134, 137, 140, 141, 142, 146, 153, 154, 155, 160
Never-ending, 101
Nevertheless, 129
Nevvy, 90
New, 53, 71, 73, 80, 113, 124, 129, 144, 152, 154, 155
Newly, 66, 74
News, 156
Newspaper, 62
Newton, 29, 54, 85, 95, 113, 130,

134, 135, 137, 145, 146, 154
Next, 46, 64, 72, 73, 97, 99, 121, 129, 134, 135, 150, 157, 158
Nice, 147, 159
Nicholas, 26, 33, 42
Nickleby, 26, 33, 42
Nigh, 105
Night, 26, 47, 72, 89, 105, 114, 131, 135, 141, 143
Nightingale, 70
Nights, 126, 133
Nine, 134, 150
Nip, 73
No, 31, 37, 38, 41, 42, 51, 54, 56, 58, 62, 67, 71, 72, 79, 82, 83, 88, 90, 91, 92, 93, 94, 95, 102, 105, 106, 109, 111, 113, 116, 117, 120, 121, 123, 124, 127, 129, 131, 133, 135, 149, 150, 158, 160
Noah, 146
Noble, 25, 61, 80
Nobly, 155
Nobody, 30
Nodded, 147
Nods, 23
Noise, 112, 156
Noisy-throated, 138
None, 112, 113, 144, 152
Nonetheless, 63
Nonsense, 24, 58
Noon, 117
Noontide, 122
Nor, 23, 60, 61, 95, 117, 141, 146, 150, 155
North, 88, 109
Northern, 109
Northrop, 120, 133, 148
Nose, 99
Nostrils, 75
Not, 20, 21, 24, 30, 36, 40, 46, 51, 53, 58, 60, 61, 63, 64, 65, 67, 69, 72, 74, 76, 78, 81, 84, 85, 87, 88, 89, 90, 92, 93, 94, 95, 96, 97, 101, 103, 104, 105, 106, 107, 108, 110, 115, 116, 117, 119, 121, 123, 125, 126, 127, 128, 129, 132, 133, 134, 135, 136, 137, 139, 142, 143, 145, 146, 147, 148, 149, 150, 151, 152, 154, 155, 156, 157, 158, 160
Notches, 97
Note, 97, 138, 155
Nothing, 25, 40, 45, 68, 79, 94, 107, 115, 117, 127, 130, 143, 147, 154, 160
Nothingness, 131
Notice, 74, 97
Noticed, 92, 131, 153
Notion, 87
Notions, 40, 131
Noun, 86
Now, 20, 40, 43, 52, 54, 57, 59, 62, 64, 65, 68, 77, 81, 86, 99, 104, 107, 109, 110, 113, 116, 119, 121, 122, 123, 126, 130, 140, 142, 146,

149, 150, 154, 155, 160
Number, 86, 116, 146
Numbers, 86, 104, 148
Numerous, 148
Nursed, 90

O

O, 54, 83, 112, 122, 141, 151
O'clock, 69, 73
Oak, 154
Object, 20, 59, 120, 127, 128
Objected, 116
Objection, 83
Obliged, 89
Observation, 39, 61
Observe, 76, 106, 117, 149
Observed, 97
Observing, 118
Occasion, 134, 154
Occasions, 133, 135
Occupation, 23
Occurred, 83, 118, 131
Occurs, 133
Ocean, 44, 76, 85, 88, 146
Oceans, 146
Och, 141
Odor, 56, 138
Of, 19, 21, 22, 24, 25, 26, 27, 28, 29, 30, 32, 33, 34, 35, 36, 37, 38, 39, 40, 42, 43, 44, 46, 47, 48, 49, 50, 51, 53, 54, 55, 56, 57, 58, 59, 60, 61, 62, 63, 64, 66, 67, 68, 69, 70, 71, 72, 73, 74, 75, 76, 77, 78, 79, 80, 81, 82, 83, 84, 85, 86, 87, 88, 89, 90, 92, 93, 94, 95, 96, 97, 98, 99, 100, 101, 102, 103, 104, 105, 106, 107, 108, 109, 110, 111, 112, 113, 114, 115, 116, 117, 118, 119, 120, 121, 123, 124, 125, 126, 127, 128, 129, 130, 131, 132, 133, 134, 135, 136, 137, 138, 139, 140, 141, 142, 143, 144, 145, 146, 147, 148, 149, 150, 151, 152, 153, 154, 155, 156, 157, 160
Off, 55, 58, 62, 67, 71, 78, 114, 135, 137, 142, 143, 145, 147, 148
Offending, 99
Office, 139
Officer, 145
Oft, 101
Often, 59, 89, 90, 98, 100, 109
Oh, 115, 136, 137
Oil-olive, 94
Old, 23, 50, 52, 73, 77, 90, 105, 116, 123, 125, 130, 140, 141, 142, 152, 153, 154
Older, 46, 119
Oldest, 134
Oliver, 23, 56
Omit, 78
On, 26, 31, 35, 36, 41, 46, 47, 51, 52, 57, 58, 59, 60, 61, 62, 63, 64, 66, 67, 71, 75, 76, 78, 89, 91, 92, 93, 95, 96, 99, 101, 102, 103, 106,

107, 109, 110, 114, 116, 117, 120, 121, 122, 124, 125, 128, 129, 130, 131, 133, 135, 136, 137, 139, 141, 142, 143, 144, 145, 146, 147, 148, 150, 152, 153, 154, 155, 156, 157, 158, 159

Once, 37, 53, 54, 89, 101, 116, 143, 151

One, 38, 57, 60, 68, 72, 74, 86, 89, 93, 95, 99, 102, 103, 104, 105, 109, 111, 112, 113, 116, 117, 118, 120, 123, 124, 125, 127, 128, 129, 130, 131, 133, 134, 135, 136, 137, 146, 148, 149, 152, 153, 154, 157, 158, 159

One's, 131

Ones, 78

Only, 30, 32, 41, 45, 49, 52, 67, 75, 76, 86, 90, 103, 106, 107, 116, 126, 147, 148, 151, 152, 153, 154, 157

Onward, 77

Open, 31, 34, 60, 61, 72, 78, 81, 93, 130, 142, 156

Openly, 135

Operations, 68, 145

Opinion, 58

Opposite, 133, 154

Or, 20, 27, 34, 37, 38, 40, 44, 48, 53, 56, 58, 60, 61, 64, 68, 70, 72, 75, 76, 79, 81, 82, 84, 86, 88, 89, 90, 93, 94, 97, 98, 100, 101, 104, 105, 107, 108, 116, 117, 124, 125, 126, 129, 130, 131, 133, 135, 137, 138, 140, 143, 144, 146, 147, 148, 151, 152, 155, 157, 160

Orchard, 122

Orchards, 79

Order, 62, 64, 93, 95, 128, 130, 148

Ordered, 139

Organized, 108

Origin, 108

Original, 51

Ornament, 68, 99

Other, 38, 40, 57, 62, 72, 83, 84, 92, 109, 110, 116, 117, 118, 120, 121, 126, 127, 133, 146, 147, 152, 153, 154

Others, 38, 59, 60, 77, 78, 84, 94, 103, 147

Otherwise, 49

Otters, 124

Ought, 88, 98, 126, 136

Our, 34, 59, 60, 62, 64, 73, 79, 84, 85, 87, 98, 102, 107, 109, 114, 120, 130, 144, 146, 155, 158

Ours, 119, 130

Out, 19, 24, 32, 50, 53, 55, 64, 72, 73, 75, 78, 80, 89, 90, 94, 95, 99, 102, 111, 113, 117, 121, 123, 124, 127, 130, 137, 138, 141, 142, 143, 145, 147, 149, 151, 152, 153, 154, 156, 157

Out-did, 101

Outdoors, 138

Outset, 120

Outside, 78, 82, 127

Outsides, 102

Oven, 82

Over, 35, 48, 58, 60, 73, 76, 77, 82, 87, 92, 101, 110, 116, 122, 124, 126, 128, 143, 147, 153

Overcame, 128

Overcast, 77

Overcoming, 120

Overhead, 142

Overladen, 121

Overlook, 142

Overset, 121

Overwhelmed, 107

Owl, 128

Own, 23, 42, 53, 81, 89, 91, 98, 128, 130, 141, 160

Owner, 123

Owners, 98

Oyster-shell, 40

Oz, 153

P

Pace, 88

Pacific, 88, 146

Padraic, 141

Page, 150, 158

Pages, 144, 152

Paid, 92, 108

Pail, 153

Painful, 59, 83

Paint, 41, 92

Painter, 92, 129, 137

Painters, 92

Painting, 41, 129

Paintings, 40

Pair, 109

Pairs, 109, 110

Palace, 135

Palatable, 139

Palm, 106

Pans, 111

Pantings, 128

Paper, 48, 51, 99

Papers, 35, 38, 48, 51, 66, 73, 79

Paramount, 83

Parchment, 130

Pardon, 145

Parents, 129

Paris, 69

Park, 20, 36, 43, 49, 68, 80

Parker, 108

Parlor, 49, 142

Part, 48, 64, 72, 90, 113, 117, 121, 126, 138, 146, 160

Participants, 140

Particular, 39, 59, 149

Particulars, 149

Parties, 133

Partly, 102, 107

Parts, 133

Pass, 81, 156

Passage, 156

Passageway, 156

Passed, 47, 73, 88, 95, 127

Passing, 144

Passion, 50

Passionate, 125

Passport, 139

Past, 87

Pastimes, 140

Pastry, 82

Pasture, 138

Path, 32, 127

Pathetically, 142

Paths, 154

Patience, 63

Patient, 29, 90

Pattern, 132

Patting, 106

Paul, 113

Pause, 87

Paws, 124

Pay, 90

Payment, 65

Peace, 103, 112, 120

Peaceable, 109

Peaceably, 109

Peaceful, 29, 144

Pearl, 40

Peartree, 122

Peasant, 108

Peculiarly, 133

Peeped, 48, 73, 99

Peg, 153

Pelf, 91

Pelicans, 148

Pelting, 31

Pendulum, 141

Penetrated, 125

Penitent, 29

Penmanship, 51

Pennies, 57, 71, 152

Pennons, 140

Penny, 57

Pensive, 101

People, 34, 41, 43, 84, 86, 89, 104, 108, 109, 118, 127, 144, 155, 156, 157

Perceived, 45

Perched, 148

Perfect, 119, 160

Perfection, 97, 133

Perfectly, 106, 117, 128

Performed, 78, 136

Perfume, 138

Perfumed, 94

Perhaps, 33, 68, 87, 139, 158

Period, 144

Perish, 107, 155

Permit, 46

Perpetually, 65

Persecute, 104

Person, 61, 86, 103, 123

Persons, 21, 104, 133

Perspiration, 145

Persuaded, 115

Pest, 46

Petted, 90

Philadelphia, 149

Phileas, 61, 139

Philosopher, 69

Philosophy, 108

Phrase, 132

Piazza, 109

Pick, 110

Pickwick, 35, 38, 48, 51, 79

Picture, 102

Pictures, 41, 92, 129

Piece, 145

Pieces, 85, 121

Pierson, 34, 37

Pies, 82

Piety, 94

Pile, 66, 141

Piled, 77, 79

Pilgrim, 70

Pilgrim's, 40

Pilgrimage, 26, 115

Pillar, 109

Pimply-faced, 48

Pinch, 151

Pine, 138, 154

Pink, 153

Pinocchio, 71, 143, 152

Pioneers, 23

Pious, 144

Piperack, 66

Pitfalls, 84

Pitiful, 142

Pity, 56

Place, 51, 56, 57, 72, 83, 85, 93, 94, 105, 114, 124, 126, 129, 135, 136, 144, 145, 155

Placed, 111

Places, 66, 89, 92, 106, 132, 135, 142

Plain, 90, 114, 117

Plan, 58

Planning, 71

Plans, 127

Planted, 54

Plants, 111, 124, 127

Plato's, 132

Play, 62, 142

Played, 143

Playground, 140

Playing, 154

Playthings, 60

Pleading, 115

Pleasant, 56, 79, 147, 158

Pleasantness, 126

Please, 60, 98, 119, 130

Pleased, 107, 115, 124, 136, 157

Pleasure, 29, 69, 101, 115

Pleasure-craft, 140

Plentiful, 64

Plentifully, 64

Pliable, 111

Plumfield, 140
Plundered, 121
Plural, 86
Poem, 26
Poet, 69, 101
Point, 36, 85, 88, 97, 120, 152
Points, 70, 100, 149
Polar, 88
Police, 135
Policemen, 135
Politics, 97
Pony, 138
Poor, 69, 71, 89, 90, 104, 118, 123, 128, 132, 152, 155, 160
Popularity, 147
Porch, 125
Portable, 121
Portion, 102, 155
Portrait, 129
Position, 63
Productive, 63
Possess, 38
Possession, 54, 131
Possessions, 116
Possible, 51, 55, 114, 119, 126, 149
Postpone, 83
Pot, 82
Potential, 93
Pouches, 148
Pounce, 109
Pounds, 148
Pour, 70
Poured, 143
Pouting, 158
Poverty, 30, 34, 142
Powder, 33
Power, 38, 49, 90, 91, 104, 133, 137, 155
Powerful, 85, 133
Practically, 51
Practice, 37, 76, 94, 140
Praise, 50, 86, 107, 136
Pray, 105
Prayed, 108
Prayer, 94, 115, 158
Prayerful, 29
Prayers, 108
Praying, 141
Precipitation, 100
Precisely, 67
Preferring, 138
Preparation, 99
Preparations, 127
Prepares, 153
Preparing, 128
Pre-Raphaelites, 129
Presence, 46
Present, 116, 119, 130
Presently, 89, 134, 148
Preserve, 95, 105
Preserved, 89
Preserving, 89
Press, 69
Pressing, 115

Pretense, 132
Pretty, 68, 82, 96, 153
Prevailed, 108
Prevails, 108
Prey, 120, 148
Preyed, 125
Pride, 145
Prided, 139
Prim, 90
Principle, 87
Print, 117, 129
Priscilla, 90
Prison, 135, 156
Prisoner, 128, 135
Prisons, 107
Privacy, 70
Private, 34
Probable, 126
Problems, 67
Proceeds, 110
Process, 59
Procure, 148
Procuring, 118
Produced, 104
Productive, 63
Profit, 118
Profiteth, 160
Progress, 32, 40, 51, 84
Promise, 40, 69, 99
Promised, 69, 147
Promises, 60
Promptly, 37
Pronoun, 86
Proper, 99, 118, 123, 132, 146, 155
Property, 116, 130, 149
Prophecies, 160
Prophecy, 160
Prophesy, 160
Proportion, 64
Proposed, 104, 149
Proposition, 155
Prospects, 114
Prosperity, 44
Protect, 90
Proud, 91, 95, 98, 145, 147
Proved, 65, 114, 147
Proverbial, 118
Proverbs, 118
Providences, 107
Province, 118
Provisions, 107
Provoked, 75, 103, 160
Prudence, 44
Prudent, 29
Psalm, 105
Public, 123, 136
Published, 118
Puddings, 82
Puffed, 160
Punt, 140
Pupil, 157
Purchase, 38
Pure, 29, 112, 144

Purely, 50, 75
Purer, 119
Purple, 66
Purpose, 21, 31, 33, 61, 66, 85, 99
Purposes, 93
Pursuit, 120, 149
Push, 145
Pushed, 142
Pushing, 120
Put, 50, 76, 82, 97, 99, 130, 135, 138, 146, 151, 152, 157, 160
Putting, 96, 99
Puzzle, 57, 116
Puzzled, 61, 96

Q

Qualify, 44
Quantity, 24, 111, 116, 131
Quarrels, 109, 110
Quarries, 142
Quarter, 55
Queen, 130
Queen's, 130
Queens, 135
Question, 75, 88, 96, 134
Questionable, 37
Questions, 134
Quick, 75, 90, 133
Quickly, 54, 115, 150, 156
Quickset, 142
Quiet, 50, 75, 114, 120, 141
Quietly, 61, 110, 139, 156
Quinet, 69
Quite, 61, 74, 84, 96, 99, 116, 127, 146, 156, 157, 158
Quivered, 77
Quivering, 70

R

Rabbit, 139
Races, 28, 140
Rackets, 140
Radiance, 99
Raft, 121
Raftered, 150
Raged, 140
Raging, 120
Railway, 139
Rain, 31, 77, 78, 87, 124, 143
Rain's, 141
Raining, 72
Raise, 145
Raised, 93
Ran, 126, 150, 153, 156
Rang, 123, 139
Ranges, 112
Rank, 34, 90
Rapid, 88
Rapidly, 104
Rapture, 122
Raptures, 91
Rash, 94
Rate, 148
Rather, 78, 88, 146, 155

Rational, 127
Rationality, 58
Ray, 156
Rays, 49
Re, 158
Reach, 50, 66, 76, 84, 126, 150
Reached, 106, 154
Reaching, 149
Read, 71, 118, 138, 144, 152, 157
Reader, 44, 57, 80, 96, 109, 110, 111, 123, 128, 149
Readiest, 90
Reading, 48
Ready, 53, 64, 153
Real, 131
Reality, 26, 131
Realize, 119, 120
Really, 30, 57, 86, 107, 130, 131, 147
Reaped, 118
Reason, 84, 103, 109, 134
Reasoned, 132
Reasons, 147
Reassured, 60
Rebuked, 123
Recall, 56
Recalling, 131
Recapture, 122
Receipt, 93
Receive, 90, 116
Received, 23, 65, 96, 116, 152
Recline, 51
Recognition, 37
Recognize, 75
Recollect, 90
Recollection, 79
Recommended, 63, 139
Record, 144
Recovery, 120
Recurred, 144
Red, 47, 73, 74, 148, 158, 159
Redheaded, 62
Redly, 77
Reduce, 86
Reeds, 152
Reedy, 138
Reef, 142
Reference, 83
References, 131
Refresh, 39
Refund, 65
Regard, 38
Regarded, 84, 100
Regardless, 42, 90
Regards, 69, 119
Regina, 130
Regular, 63
Regularly, 133
Reign, 55
Rejoice, 105, 144
Rejoiced, 136
Rejoiceth, 160
Relates, 128
Relation, 108

Released, 135
Reliance, 83
Relief, 53, 119
Relieved, 53
Religion, 108
Reluctant, 60, 147
Remaining, 126, 155
Remains, 88
Remark, 75
Remarkable, 118
Remember, 62, 79, 125, 134, 138, 139, 155
Remembered, 95, 120, 134
Remembrance, 46
Remembrances, 56
Remind, 86
Remove, 126, 160
Removed, 137
Renames, 86
Render, 126
Rendered, 111
Renewed, 89
Renown, 91
Repair, 102
Repaired, 139
Repairing, 145
Repassed, 47
Repeated, 133, 134
Replace, 86
Replied, 88, 139, 145, 159
Reply, 75
Represent, 103
Representing, 80
Reproduce, 92
Requested, 65
Require, 147
Resembling, 133
Resided, 102
Resigned, 115
Resinous, 138
Resolve, 97, 155
Resolved, 55, 104, 126, 149
Resources, 114
Respected, 116
Responsibility, 108
Rest, 60, 121, 148
Restaurant, 62
Rested, 137
Resting, 155
Restless, 33
Restored, 128
Result, 59, 63
Results, 87, 108
Retain, 67
Retained, 67
Retard, 51
Retarded, 108
Retrospect, 144
Return, 58, 88, 89, 106, 109, 154
Returned, 154
Revealed, 124
Reverently, 87
Reviewed, 144
Revolution, 80, 145

Rewarded, 152
Ribbons, 35
Ribs, 140
Rice, 64, 82
Rich, 61, 79, 131, 142
Richard, 29, 54, 85, 95, 113, 118, 130, 134, 135, 137, 145, 146, 154
Richard's, 118
Riches, 61, 93
Ride, 89
Right, 50, 62, 66, 80, 84, 85, 88, 93, 103, 106, 147
Righteous, 105
Right-hand, 102
Rights, 123
Rime, 47
Ring, 79, 123
Riot, 142
Rip, 100
Rip's, 100
Rippling, 56
Rise, 108
Rising, 53, 114, 117, 149
River, 81, 140, 148
Roach, 127
Road, 96, 141, 150
Roads, 106, 141
Roam, 70
Roar, 133
Roaring, 105, 133
Roars, 133
Rob, 90
Robert, 122, 150
Robin, 74, 109, 110
Robins, 110, 111
Robinson, 53, 64, 72, 76, 78, 82, 97, 107, 114, 117, 121, 126, 144
Rock, 81
Rocking, 45
Rocks, 107, 156
Rod, 149
Rode, 89, 145
Rogue, 139
Rolling, 73, 152
Roof, 102
Roofs, 73
Room, 99, 117
Rooting, 54
Rope, 123, 150
Rose, 112, 140
Rotted, 123
Rough, 68, 74, 122, 137
Round, 67, 74, 82, 88, 113, 117, 122, 127, 134, 146, 148, 154
Rouse, 44
Roused, 99, 114
Route, 127
Row, 99
Rowed, 140
Royal, 130
Rubbish, 137
Ruddy, 52
Ruin, 102
Rule, 86, 104, 116

Rumbling, 77
Run, 151
Rung, 123
Running, 124
Rush, 85, 87
Rustling, 138, 158

S

Sack, 118
Sacred, 139
Sad, 111, 119
Sadness, 144
Safe, 89, 140, 159
Safety, 89
Said, 41, 62, 68, 71, 88, 91, 98, 105, 106, 123, 124, 132, 134, 137, 139, 144, 145, 147, 149, 150, 153, 154, 157, 158, 159
Sail, 88
Sailing, 35, 77
Sails, 143
Saint, 147
Saints, 50
Sake, 103, 112
Salary, 129
Salesman, 65
Salt, 107
Saluted, 114
Salvaging, 121
Same, 28, 55, 57, 61, 88, 93, 103, 104, 109, 110, 116, 126, 128, 133
Sand, 85, 117, 143
Sanders, 44, 154
Sandwich, 62
Sat, 47
Satan, 94
Satisfied, 39, 87, 152
Saturn, 132
Sauce, 139
Saunders, 118
Save, 77, 106, 140, 143, 152
Saved, 78
Saving, 87
Savior, 113
Savor, 94
Saw, 46, 54, 74, 81, 99, 101, 107, 124, 136, 137, 143, 148, 153, 156, 157, 159
Sawyer, 131
Say, 28, 46, 64, 68, 71, 78, 86, 93, 96, 98, 117, 119, 130, 147, 151, 155
Scaffolding, 102
Scampered, 156
Scarce, 60, 118, 126
Scarcely, 118
Scatters, 122
Scenery, 73
Scenes, 56
Scent, 74, 75
Schell, 41, 129
Scheme, 76
Scholars, 132

School, 71, 128, 129, 157
Schoolhouse, 157
Science, 51, 149
Scientific, 140
Score, 155
Scotland, 83, 151
Scott, 91
Scottish, 133
Scoured, 100
Scrapes, 90
Scraps, 124
Screams, 140
Screens, 142
Scrooge, 31
Sculptor, 137
Sea, 35, 44, 76, 88, 107, 142, 143
Seacoast, 126
Seal, 130
Search, 103
Searched, 143
Seas, 88
Seaside, 126
Season, 26, 66, 79, 87, 89, 92, 115
Seat, 48, 66
Seated, 138
Second, 66, 106, 126, 150
Secondhand, 152
Seconds, 53
Secrecy, 127
Secret, 27, 74, 115, 124, 127
Secrets, 142
Secure, 29, 72, 112, 126
Secured, 23
Securing, 118
See, 62, 71, 74, 76, 85, 86, 90, 92, 106, 109, 117, 123, 124, 127, 135, 137, 143, 147, 148, 150, 154, 160
Seed, 54, 87
Seeding, 142
Seeds, 138
Seedy, 66
Seeing, 144
Seeketh, 160
Seem, 52, 56, 81, 127
Seemed, 33, 48, 50, 55, 58, 61, 75, 77, 99, 107, 110, 111, 129, 131, 136, 140, 142
Seemingly, 109
Seems, 93, 133, 134, 147
Seen, 64, 88, 93, 97, 107, 117, 131, 142, 148, 156
Sees, 83, 122
Seized, 58, 156
Selah, 105
Selected, 110
Selects, 110
Self, 91
Self-gratification, 21
Seller, 65
Send, 135, 145
Sending, 94, 123
Sensation, 55, 128
Sense, 42, 98, 132, 136, 155
Sent, 58, 92

Sentence, 86
Sentences, 118
Sentiment, 48
Sentiments, 108
Sentinels, 148
Sentry, 112
Separation, 99
Serenity, 55
Serious, 124, 127, 132
Serve, 90, 98, 113
Served, 139
Service, 94, 123
Serving, 49
Set, 58, 73, 82, 90, 106, 107, 111, 113, 128, 153
Settle, 88, 110
Settled, 129
Seven, 104, 106, 116, 125, 155
Sevens, 104
Seventh, 134
Several, 66, 82, 89, 140, 148
Severe, 128
Sewell, 98
Shabby, 142
Shade, 138, 144
Shades, 136
Shady, 70
Shaken, 58
Shakespeare, 59
Shall, 27, 46, 50, 57, 71, 91, 94, 105, 106, 113, 123, 134, 136, 155, 160
Shalt, 105
Shaped, 88
Share, 52
Shares, 116
Sharp, 52
Sharply, 123
Sharp-pointed, 149
She, 30, 36, 39, 43, 49, 55, 58, 69, 74, 98, 128, 132, 145, 153
Sheaf, 122
Sheaves, 79
Sheet, 130
Shelf, 141, 153
Shelter, 114, 123
Sherlock, 62, 66, 67, 73, 75, 83, 102, 106
Shield, 95
Shilling, 30
Shine, 101
Shining, 73, 74, 141, 148
Ship, 64, 88, 121
Ships, 81, 85
Shirtsleeves, 71
Shoes, 132, 153
Shone, 75, 77
Shoo, 129
Shook, 158
Shoot, 53, 78
Shop, 62, 77, 129
Shopkeeper, 65
Shore, 53, 64, 76, 117, 121
Short, 61, 115, 152, 156

Should, 41, 62, 67, 69, 72, 83, 86, 90, 98, 103, 113, 114, 116, 122, 123, 126, 129, 130, 132, 135, 140, 144, 151, 155, 156, 159
Shoulders, 75
Shout, 105
Show, 81, 101, 116, 120, 130, 153
Showed, 102, 128
Shown, 63
Shrill, 140
Shrubbery, 68, 127
Shut, 94
Sick, 116
Sickle, 79
Sickly, 49
Sickness, 89
Side, 35, 68, 102, 106, 110, 148, 154
Sidelong, 100
Sides, 154
Sideways, 51
Sighs, 133
Sight, 50, 55, 81, 99, 143
Sign, 130
Signal, 154
Signature, 130
Signs, 67, 102, 125
Silence, 105
Silent, 38, 56, 81
Silken, 150
Silky, 138
Silly, 158
Silver, 71
Simon, 83
Simple, 57, 86, 142
Simplest, 96
Simply, 104, 127, 132
Sin, 37, 105
Since, 39, 46, 74, 89, 97
Sincere, 119
Sinewy, 75
Sing, 138
Singing, 109, 133
Sings, 122
Singular, 86
Sins, 104
Sir, 32, 62, 66, 67, 73, 75, 83, 91, 102, 106, 139, 145, 157
Sisters, 99
Sit, 106
Sits, 112
Sitting, 68, 96, 120, 134, 153
Situation, 114, 120
Six, 104, 133
Sixpence, 30
Sixteen, 58, 64
Size, 146
Sketch, 100
Skies, 79
Skill, 44, 137
Skillful, 44, 112
Skins, 78
Skip, 74
Skipped, 74

Skipping-rope, 74
Sky, 35, 47, 70, 73, 77, 81, 85, 92, 142, 143, 148
Skylark, 70
Slate, 157
Sleep, 52, 56, 60, 114, 131
Sleepy, 158, 159
Slender, 140
Slept, 49, 114
Slight, 67
Slipped, 142
Slipping, 150
Slow, 19, 59, 150
Slowly, 41, 102
Slumber, 142
Small, 37, 45, 48, 85, 90, 129, 140, 143, 146
Smaller, 47, 85, 156
Smallest, 67
Smart, 96
Smell, 55, 138
Smiled, 56, 158, 159
Smiles, 50, 112
Smiling, 106, 132
Smoke, 102
Smokeless, 81
Smooth, 44, 154
Snapped, 47
Snarl, 75
Sneaked, 100
Sneered, 132
Snort, 138
Snow, 31, 79, 154
Snowballing, 154
So, 19, 25, 32, 34, 39, 43, 45, 51, 53, 57, 60, 61, 62, 69, 72, 75, 76, 78, 81, 82, 85, 91, 92, 94, 95, 100, 103, 104, 107, 111, 119, 121, 124, 125, 126, 131, 132, 133, 135, 139, 142, 143, 144, 145, 146, 147, 150, 152, 153, 154, 155, 157, 158, 159, 160
Soak, 63
Soaked, 111
Soar, 70
Social, 108
Society, 34, 147
Socket, 146
Sods, 141
Sofa, 66
Soft, 138
Softer, 55
Softly, 47
Softly-colored, 92
Soil, 54, 108
Sold, 152
Soldier, 95
Soldiers, 145
Sole, 100
Solemn, 133
Solitary, 54
Solitude, 101
Solon, 29
Some, 51, 54, 56, 62, 78, 83, 90,

94, 95, 102, 103, 104, 107, 111, 119, 121, 122, 126, 129, 135, 136, 137, 140, 142, 145, 149, 152, 153, 154, 156
Something, 33, 125, 126, 130, 147, 156, 157
Sometimes, 56, 61, 89, 107, 124, 126, 134
Somewhat, 63, 86, 131, 153
Son, 90, 93, 116
Song, 122
Songs, 105, 108
Sons, 116, 144
Soon, 39, 55, 77, 88, 94, 106, 150, 156
Soothingly, 106
Sorely, 63
Sorrow, 25, 87, 119
Sorrows, 105
Sort, 48, 119
Soughing, 138
Sought, 108
Soul, 22, 50, 81, 91, 112, 113, 115, 136, 147
Souls, 28
Sound, 29, 52, 114
Sounding, 160
Sounds, 86, 133
Source, 104
Southern, 125, 142
Sown, 54
Space, 41
Spaces, 118
Spake, 160
Spaniards, 64
Sparkling, 101, 153
Spartans, 156
Spattered, 106
Spatters, 106
Speak, 54, 84, 136, 160
Speaking, 23, 130
Special, 136
Specially, 147
Speckled, 141
Spectacle, 99
Sped, 158
Speech, 84, 131
Spend, 135, 144
Spent, 92, 124, 126, 129, 135
Spiced, 139
Spicy, 138
Spider, 150, 151
Spill, 128
Spirit, 92, 100, 105, 142
Spite, 33, 67, 87, 147
Splendid, 60, 131
Splendor, 81, 143
Split, 140
Spoil, 98, 127
Sport, 26
Sports, 140, 158
Spot, 143, 148, 151
Sprang, 54, 156
Sprawl, 150

Spray's, 122
Spread, 77, 107, 153
Sprightly, 101
Spring, 73, 79, 92, 109, 110, 125, 158
Sprinkling, 33
Spritsail-yard, 121
Spruce, 110
Sprung, 91
Spurred, 143
Squad, 145
Square, 80
Squares, 123
Squeeze, 156
Squirrels, 124
St., 83, 147
Stags, 133
Stains, 49
Stake, 128
Staked, 126
Stammered, 59
Stand, 118, 157
Standing, 62, 76, 80, 154
Stands, 45, 80, 110, 112
Stanley, 120
Stanley's, 120
Stare, 24
Stared, 106
Stars, 101, 112
Start, 106, 154
Started, 106, 129, 154
Startled, 156
Startles, 133
Starvation, 156
Starve, 123
Starving, 123, 152
State, 108
Stated, 130
States, 104
Statesman, 97
Station, 106, 131, 139
Statue, 80
Stay, 38, 60, 132, 150, 158
Stayed, 72
Staying, 134
Stead, 60
Steadily, 144, 151
Steady, 98, 150
Steely, 75, 142
Steep, 81
Stench, 94
Step, 32, 59
Steps, 90, 117, 125
Stern, 26
Stick, 152
Sticks, 78
Stifling, 49
Stile, 96
Still, 49, 53, 60, 70, 81, 84, 98, 120, 142, 150, 153, 156
Stir, 72
Stirred, 56, 148
Stitches, 90
Stock, 116

Stone, 102, 137
Stonework, 102
Stood, 75, 108, 117, 125, 145, 154
Stool, 141
Stopped, 134, 137, 150
Store, 63, 64, 90, 93, 141
Storm, 35, 55, 77
Storms, 44
Story, 59, 84, 95, 123, 125, 128, 135, 138, 144, 149
Straight, 150, 154
Straightest, 154
Strain, 56, 140
Strand, 91
Stranded, 114
Strange, 98, 104, 110, 124, 133, 156
Stranger, 134, 145
Straw, 124, 143
Stream, 148
Streaming, 156
Street, 75, 80
Strengthened, 144
Stretch, 32, 143
Stretched, 78, 80, 101
Striking, 133
String, 97
Stripped, 142
Strive, 50, 150
Strong, 42, 126, 131, 142, 143, 144, 150, 152
Stronger, 152
Strongest, 85
Strongly, 49
Struck, 68
Struggle, 87, 125
Struggled, 155
Student, 128
Studied, 66, 132, 138, 152
Studies, 152
Studio, 137
Studious, 29
Study, 124
Stuffed, 128
Stumbling, 103
Stump, 117
Subdued, 131
Subject, 72, 149
Submarine, 88
Subservient, 29
Subsist, 148
Substitute, 22
Suburban, 62
Succeeded, 116, 125, 144, 152
Success, 44, 87
Successful, 154
Succession, 133
Such, 37, 43, 51, 55, 58, 63, 75, 79, 90, 91, 93, 95, 96, 97, 99, 101, 104, 113, 118, 119, 121, 126, 127, 128, 129, 131, 133, 137, 144, 145, 149, 153, 158
Sudden, 56, 58
Suddenly, 156

Suffer, 115
Suffered, 89, 135
Suffereth, 160
Sufferings, 128
Sufficient, 127
Suggested, 66
Suggestion, 138
Suit, 78, 137, 152
Suited, 144
Sullivan, 125
Sum, 93, 104, 131, 135
Summer, 55, 105, 142
Summers, 109
Sums, 131
Sun, 26, 49, 50, 55, 73, 74, 77, 78, 81, 85, 88, 99, 107, 125, 143
Sun's, 49
Sunbonnet, 153
Sunday, 96
Sung, 108
Sunlight, 156
Sunlit, 138
Sunny, 152
Sunrise, 92
Sunset, 92
Sunshine, 49, 87
Superintending, 145
Superstitions, 104
Supplicating, 128
Supplied, 43, 61, 77
Supplies, 107, 120
Support, 129
Suppose, 84, 113, 130
Supposed, 131
Supposing, 82
Sure, 29, 43, 87, 90, 96, 119, 134, 141, 147, 150
Surely, 37, 105, 153
Surface, 53
Surprise, 107, 125
Surprised, 117, 137, 157
Surround, 72
Surrounded, 126
Surrounding, 127
Survey, 48
Susan, 158
Suspect, 127
Suspended, 66, 109
Suspicion, 20
Swallows, 122
Swam, 143
Swarm, 29, 159
Swear, 139
Sweep, 59
Sweeping, 82, 141, 148
Sweeps, 79
Sweet, 81, 94, 112, 119, 125, 128
Sweeten, 107
Sweetly, 47, 115
Sweetness, 62
Sweet-smelling, 79
Swell, 91
Swiftness, 53
Swim, 53

Swimming, 143, 148
Swinging, 141
Swinton's, 80, 109, 110, 111, 123, 128, 149
Swiss, 114, 144
Sword, 80
Swung, 150, 158
Syllable, 59
Sympathy, 38, 129
System, 84

T

Tabernacle, 94
Table, 57, 107, 134
Taciturn, 61
Tail, 100, 153, 156
Tailor, 78
Take, 40, 86, 87, 88, 97, 111, 113, 114, 144, 145, 152, 155, 157
Taken, 54, 89, 90, 95, 99, 129, 135, 146
Takes, 60, 119, 134
Taking, 96, 116, 133, 145, 153
Tale, 144, 151
Talent, 36
Talk, 124
Talked, 24, 61
Talking, 71, 74
Talks, 127
Tall, 80, 154
Tangle, 65
Tarry, 115
Task, 51, 155
Taste, 36
Tasted, 139
Taught, 138
Tax, 108
Teach, 98, 105
Teacher, 125, 157
Teachers, 84
Tears, 50
Tedious, 89
Tell, 33, 108, 135, 151, 154, 157, 158
Tells, 52, 83, 123, 146
Temperate, 29
Temples, 81
Tempt, 93
Tempting, 126
Ten, 101, 118, 144, 147
Tender, 90
Tennis, 140
Tent, 114
Terms, 147
Terrific, 87
Terrified, 117
Terror, 128
Terrors, 100
Test, 96
Testament, 113
Testing, 155
Than, 31, 36, 40, 41, 46, 58, 63, 74, 78, 79, 84, 85, 86, 98, 104,

106, 109, 113, 116, 119, 120, 122, 128, 129, 144, 146, 152

Thank, 63

Thankful, 22, 37, 87

Thankfulness, 115

Thanks, 69, 87, 90

That, 24, 25, 30, 31, 33, 34, 38, 39, 40, 41, 42, 45, 46, 49, 53, 54, 56, 57, 58, 59, 60, 61, 62, 63, 64, 65, 66, 67, 69, 70, 71, 72, 75, 76, 78, 79, 81, 83, 84, 85, 86, 87, 88, 90, 92, 93, 94, 95, 96, 97, 98, 99, 101, 102, 103, 104, 105, 106, 107, 109, 110, 111, 112, 113, 114, 115, 116, 117, 118, 119, 120, 121, 122, 123, 125, 126, 127, 128, 129, 130, 131, 134, 135, 136, 137, 138, 139, 140, 142, 143, 144, 145, 146, 147, 148, 149, 150, 151, 152, 153, 154, 155, 157, 160

That's, 122, 134

The, 19, 22, 23, 24, 25, 26, 27, 28, 29, 30, 32, 34, 35, 36, 38, 39, 40, 42, 43, 44, 45, 46, 47, 48, 49, 50, 51, 52, 53, 54, 55, 56, 57, 58, 59, 60, 61, 62, 63, 64, 65, 66, 67, 68, 69, 70, 71, 72, 73, 74, 75, 76, 77, 78, 79, 80, 81, 82, 83, 84, 85, 86, 87, 88, 89, 90, 91, 92, 93, 94, 95, 96, 97, 98, 99, 100, 101, 102, 103, 104, 105, 106, 107, 108, 109, 110, 111, 112, 113, 114, 115, 116, 117, 118, 119, 120, 121, 122, 123, 124, 125, 126, 127, 128, 129, 130, 131, 132, 133, 134, 135, 136, 137, 138, 139, 140, 141, 142, 143, 144, 145, 146, 147, 148, 149, 150, 151, 152, 153, 154, 155, 156, 157, 158, 159, 160

Theaters, 81

Thee, 50, 105, 112

Their, 26, 28, 34, 45, 60, 62, 71, 79, 90, 92, 93, 95, 98, 99, 101, 108, 109, 110, 120, 127, 132, 133, 134, 135, 138, 140, 141, 142, 144, 145, 147, 148, 154, 155, 158

Them, 35, 45, 57, 59, 60, 73, 75, 78, 82, 85, 86, 90, 99, 100, 101, 104, 110, 116, 119, 124, 127, 134, 135, 138, 143, 144, 145, 146, 148, 152, 154, 156, 157, 159

Themselves, 51, 93, 95, 98, 124, 127, 129, 142, 148

Then, 54, 57, 62, 67, 69, 71, 77, 82, 85, 101, 106, 112, 113, 114, 130, 131, 134, 135, 137, 143, 145, 148, 153, 154, 156, 157, 160

Theodore, 108

There, 24, 25, 32, 33, 34, 35, 36, 40, 43, 45, 47, 49, 58, 62, 63, 67, 72, 73, 76, 77, 79, 82, 85, 91, 92, 94, 97, 98, 102, 105, 106, 112, 113, 116, 117, 120, 122, 123, 124, 126, 129, 131, 135, 136, 141, 143,

145, 146, 147, 149, 150, 151, 153, 154, 160

There's, 137, 141, 147

Thereby, 115, 118

Therefore, 67, 83, 84, 96, 99, 104, 118, 126, 146

These, 40, 51, 56, 72, 78, 92, 98, 102, 111, 113, 116, 120, 121, 134, 144, 146, 149, 155, 160

They, 28, 40, 50, 55, 57, 59, 68, 77, 78, 79, 85, 90, 95, 97, 98, 101, 104, 105, 107, 108, 109, 110, 111, 113, 115, 116, 124, 127, 129, 131, 132, 133, 135, 137, 138, 142, 143, 145, 147, 148, 149, 153, 154, 155, 156, 159, 160

Thick, 79

Thine, 70

Thing, 27, 49, 57, 61, 74, 78, 94, 97, 107, 120, 126, 127, 147, 150, 158

Things, 25, 40, 43, 52, 63, 71, 85, 89, 120, 124, 133, 135, 138, 142, 146, 147, 152, 160

Think, 72, 86, 92, 95, 96, 98, 107, 111, 122, 124, 127, 134, 136, 138, 157

Thinker, 75

Thinketh, 160

Thinking, 150

Thinks, 83

Third, 125, 133

Thirst, 156

Thirty, 53

This, 27, 28, 32, 36, 40, 41, 43, 46, 52, 56, 65, 66, 67, 68, 71, 75, 76, 78, 79, 80, 81, 82, 83, 84, 85, 86, 88, 89, 91, 92, 93, 95, 96, 97, 99, 102, 103, 105, 106, 107, 109, 110, 111, 113, 116, 119, 120, 121, 122, 123, 125, 126, 127, 129, 130, 131, 133, 134, 135, 137, 139, 140, 144, 145, 149, 152, 155, 156

Thistle, 54

Thistles, 54

Thither, 112, 117

Thomas, 132, 154

Thoroughly, 114

Those, 40, 54, 61, 70, 88, 91, 92, 93, 107, 118, 135, 144, 151, 155

Thou, 70, 94, 105, 112

Though, 40, 53, 56, 60, 63, 64, 91, 97, 103, 107, 113, 121, 122, 126, 147, 160

Thought, 48, 59, 68, 94, 96, 97, 101, 126, 127, 142, 145, 154, 160

Thoughtful, 29, 98

Thoughts, 94, 107, 117, 126, 144

Thousand, 88, 101, 118

Thousands, 92, 131, 148

Thrashed, 64

Thread, 150

Threat, 93

Threatened, 46

Threatening, 142

Three, 49, 57, 68, 76, 97, 109, 110, 116, 117, 125, 126, 133, 156, 157, 160

Threw, 23, 73, 121, 137

Throng, 42

Through, 21, 26, 60, 77, 95, 105, 137, 138, 156, 158, 160

Throwing, 124, 145

Thrown, 102

Throws, 106

Thrush, 110, 122

Thumbnail, 41

Thunder, 77, 133

Thundered, 143

Thunderstorm, 77

Thunderstruck, 117

Thus, 56, 68, 76, 82, 88, 129, 136, 151, 155

Thy, 70, 94, 105, 112

Ticket, 106

Ticking, 141

Tide, 121, 148

Tied, 123, 128, 153

Till, 69, 82, 134, 136, 137, 142, 145, 150, 154, 156, 159

Timber, 145

Time, 29, 41, 46, 53, 54, 62, 68, 72, 76, 79, 80, 82, 83, 85, 87, 88, 89, 92, 93, 103, 105, 109, 115, 116, 119, 123, 126, 127, 131, 133, 137, 139, 143, 144, 145, 148, 149, 150, 151, 152, 156, 158

Times, 95, 131, 133

Tinges, 79

Tinkling, 160

Tints, 92

Tiny, 85, 122, 124

Tips, 90

Tire, 76, 150

Tired, 141

Title, 130

Titles, 91

To, 20, 21, 22, 24, 29, 30, 31, 32, 33, 34, 36, 37, 39, 40, 41, 43, 45, 46, 48, 49, 50, 51, 52, 53, 54, 55, 56, 57, 58, 59, 60, 61, 62, 63, 64, 65, 67, 68, 69, 70, 71, 72, 73, 74, 75, 76, 77, 78, 79, 80, 81, 82, 83, 84, 85, 86, 87, 88, 89, 90, 91, 92, 93, 94, 95, 96, 97, 98, 99, 100, 101, 103, 104, 105, 107, 108, 109, 110, 111, 112, 113, 114, 115, 116, 117, 118, 119, 120, 121, 122, 123, 124, 125, 126, 127, 128, 129, 130, 131, 132, 133, 134, 135, 136, 137, 138, 139, 140, 141, 142, 143, 144, 145, 146, 147, 148, 149, 150, 151, 152, 153, 154, 155, 156, 157, 158, 159, 160

Toad's, 40

Tobacconist, 62

Today, 71, 96, 157

Toes, 117

Together, 68, 104, 109, 114, 126, 133, 152, 157

Toiled, 123

Toiling, 35

Toils, 136, 150

Told, 43, 54, 69, 95, 98, 135, 144, 146

Tom, 36, 131

Tom's, 131

Tomorrow, 69, 71, 96, 147

Tongue, 51, 100

Tongues, 160

Too, 40, 60, 63, 71, 84, 90, 96, 97, 107, 131, 140, 146, 154, 156

Took, 48, 124, 126, 132, 143, 145, 153, 157

Tools, 97, 108

Toothbrush, 63

Top, 48, 57, 76, 145, 149, 153

Tops, 124

Tormented, 131

Torture, 128

Tossed, 143

Tossing, 101

Totally, 49

Toto, 153

Touch, 57

Touches, 57, 88

Touching, 81, 128

Tour, 76, 88

Toward, 74, 80

Towards, 47, 53, 76, 117, 142, 147, 148, 154, 156

Tower, 123, 149

Towers, 81

Town, 49, 123

Track, 154

Tracks, 154

Traditions, 28

Traffic, 97

Trail, 75

Train, 77, 106

Training, 144

Traits, 90

Tranquil, 55

Transacted, 139

Transactions, 108

Transcends, 60

Transferred, 116

Transformed, 75

Transgression, 105

Transgressions, 105

Transition, 55

Transparent, 29

Transported, 127

Trap, 59

Trapping, 59

Travel, 153

Travelers, 139

Traveling, 58

Traversed, 59

Tread, 150

Treasure, 131

Treat, 107, 116

Treated, 98
Tree, 109, 110, 117, 138, 154, 158, 159
Trees, 47, 79, 80, 101, 124, 138, 148, 153
Trembling, 136
Tremendous, 143
Triangle, 57, 148
Tribes, 120
Trick, 142
Tried, 63, 129, 143, 149, 151, 157
Trilled, 138
Trim, 140
Triumphs, 128
Troop, 133
Troops, 133
Tropics, 120, 133, 148
Trouble, 84, 98, 105, 135
Troublesome, 54
Trousers, 48
Trout, 124
True, 21, 22, 29, 70, 100, 119
Truly, 63
Trust, 24, 69, 136
Trusteth, 105
Trustful, 29
Truth, 54, 103, 160
Try, 57, 69, 151, 157
Trying, 92, 95, 113, 123, 140, 145
Tugging, 123
Tulip, 138
Tumbled, 110
Tumbles, 150
Turf, 141
Turn, 50, 54, 97, 123, 127, 154
Turned, 38, 74, 91, 105, 120, 123, 127, 143
Turning, 145
Turnip, 157
Twain, 131
Twelve, 129
Twenty, 53, 64, 88, 149
Twenty-five, 118
Twenty-one, 113, 116
Twenty-two, 64
Twice, 58, 122
Twig, 143
Twinkle, 101
Twist, 56
Two, 53, 64, 75, 76, 86, 102, 107, 109, 110, 116, 117, 121, 125, 126, 133, 134, 147
Type, 70

U

Ugly, 54
Ultimate, 67
Unaware, 122
Unawares, 119
Unconsciously, 125
Undecorated, 142
Under, 71, 88, 104, 118, 136, 140, 155
Understand, 60, 113, 160

Understanding, 39, 105
Understood, 160
Undertaking, 120
Undoubtedly, 61
Uneasiness, 43
Unfinished, 155
Unfit, 94
Ungraspable, 131
Unhappy, 126
Unhealthful, 120
Unheeded, 75
Unhonored, 91
Uniform, 80
Uninterrupted, 44
Union, 44, 80
Unit, 42
United, 144
Unknown, 60, 67, 124, 135
Unless, 130
Unlocks, 34
Unnecessary, 67
Unpleasant, 43
Unquestionably, 51
Unseemly, 160
Unselfish, 58
Unshapen, 137
Unsheath, 124
Unsung, 91
Untied, 128
Until, 41, 59, 67, 74, 111, 127, 138, 158
Unto, 81, 105
Unusual, 125
Unwept, 91
Unwieldy, 121
Up, 35, 45, 53, 54, 56, 65, 69, 74, 77, 78, 85, 98, 99, 102, 103, 106, 107, 110, 117, 124, 126, 127, 128, 133, 135, 139, 141, 145, 148, 150, 151, 152, 153, 156, 157, 160
Uplift, 99
Upon, 31, 33, 47, 53, 66, 70, 73, 75, 76, 77, 81, 82, 83, 96, 97, 100, 101, 105, 107, 109, 116, 125, 126, 127, 129, 130, 139, 141, 145, 158, 159
Upper, 68
Upright, 105, 118
Upturned, 125
Urge, 158
Us, 22, 27, 34, 38, 52, 60, 62, 64, 69, 85, 87, 88, 92, 98, 107, 108, 113, 114, 120, 130, 134, 146, 148, 149, 154, 155, 158
Use, 50, 59, 85, 93, 99, 103, 107, 118, 121, 134, 137, 138, 149, 154
Used, 41, 129, 135, 140, 152
Useful, 61, 78, 108, 118
Usefulness, 44, 144
Utensils, 63
Utterly, 42

V

Vacant, 101
Vague, 131

Vaguely, 125
Vain, 98, 155
Vales, 101
Valley, 81, 84
Valuable, 68
Value, 116
Valueless, 65
Van Winkle, 100
Van Winkle's, 100
Vanish, 56, 160
Varied, 23, 140
Various, 65, 124
Vast, 24, 59, 88, 131, 148
Vaughan, 112
Vaunteth, 160
Vegetable-diet, 48
Vegetarian, 62
Vehicle, 106, 118
Veil, 77
Veins, 75
Vending, 118
Verily, 103
Verne, 61, 88, 139
Verse, 113
Very, 30, 33, 34, 41, 42, 51, 53, 58, 61, 64, 66, 68, 69, 71, 73, 78, 81, 82, 83, 89, 95, 97, 111, 117, 120, 121, 126, 129, 131, 133, 135, 143, 151, 152, 156, 157, 158
Vessel, 35
Vex, 62
Victoria, 130
Victualled, 64
Vie, 133
View, 58, 126
Vigilant, 114
Vile, 91
Village, 96, 154
Vine, 123
Violent, 106
Violin-land, 62
Virtue, 118
Visit, 102, 134
Visitor, 52
Visitors, 148
Voice, 114, 133
Voices, 47, 133
Void, 40, 77
Volume, 152
Voluntary, 56
Voyage, 64, 121
Voyager, 44

W

Wabble, 140
Wadsworth, 60
Wage, 93
Wagged, 153
Waistcoat, 78
Waited, 125, 157
Waiting, 159
Wakefulness, 131
Wakes, 122

Waking, 94
Walk, 68, 74, 96, 127, 154
Walked, 71, 102
Walking, 137
Walks, 127
Wall, 72, 102, 141
Walls, 127
Walter, 91
Wandered, 101, 123
Wandering, 91
Want, 86, 93, 98, 118, 136, 142, 158
Wanted, 74, 107, 129, 143, 152, 153
Wanting, 78
War, 108, 127, 145, 155
Warehouse, 129
Warm, 31, 55, 78, 142, 152, 159
Warmest, 90
Warmth, 31, 58
Warn, 93
Warning, 92
Wars, 112, 120
Was, 20, 31, 33, 35, 36, 39, 41, 43, 46, 47, 48, 49, 53, 54, 55, 58, 59, 61, 64, 65, 66, 68, 71, 72, 73, 74, 75, 76, 77, 78, 82, 84, 85, 88, 92, 95, 96, 97, 98, 99, 100, 102, 104, 105, 107, 109, 111, 113, 114, 115, 116, 117, 118, 120, 121, 123, 124, 125, 126, 127, 128, 129, 130, 131, 135, 136, 137, 139, 140, 142, 143, 144, 145, 146, 147, 148, 149, 150, 152, 153, 154, 156, 157, 160
Washed, 153
Washings, 153
Washington, 80, 100
Waste, 116
Wasted, 131
Wasting, 137
Watch, 76, 104
Watched, 124, 156
Watching, 124
Water, 23, 53, 56, 111, 121, 128, 146, 148, 152, 153
Water-insects, 148
Water-rats, 124
Waters, 35, 88, 105, 143, 146
Wave, 53, 143
Waves, 85, 101, 143
Waving, 79
Waxed, 105
Way, 53, 73, 76, 88, 95, 101, 105, 106, 111, 124, 135, 141, 142, 146, 147, 150, 154, 156, 157, 158
Ways, 50, 95, 124
We, 34, 38, 59, 60, 62, 64, 67, 68, 69, 73, 79, 84, 85, 87, 88, 92, 97, 106, 109, 113, 114, 117, 129, 130, 134, 138, 144, 146, 148, 149, 154, 155, 158, 160
We've, 62
Weak, 156
Wealth, 38, 91, 101, 118

Weapons, 108
Wear, 66, 81
Weariness, 87
Wears, 79
Weary, 115, 141
Weather, 31, 55, 132
Weatherstaff, 74
Webbed, 148
Wedding, 83
Weeds, 54
Week, 24, 43, 96, 97
Weeks, 125
Weights, 141
Welcome, 90
Welcoming, 23
Welfare, 144
Well, 67, 73, 78, 82, 86, 88, 91, 108, 111, 126, 130, 138, 139, 140, 146, 147, 157
Went, 65, 77, 88, 96, 117, 121, 125, 129, 135, 136, 137, 150, 151, 152, 153, 157
Were, 19, 33, 36, 55, 56, 59, 61, 67, 68, 73, 74, 75, 78, 89, 93, 97, 102, 103, 109, 111, 114, 116, 117, 120, 124, 127, 130, 131, 134, 137, 139, 140, 142, 143, 145, 146, 147, 148, 150, 152, 153, 154, 156
West, 73
Westminster, 81
What, 21, 22, 40, 60, 67, 68, 72, 79, 84, 92, 93, 96, 99, 100, 101, 103, 104, 107, 108, 113, 119, 121, 123, 125, 134, 135, 139, 143, 148, 149, 150, 153, 154, 155, 156, 157
What's, 137
Whatever, 34, 59, 61
Wheel, 97
Whelming, 82
When, 23, 38, 42, 46, 50, 53, 60, 67, 75, 79, 82, 84, 85, 87, 92, 95, 96, 99, 101, 105, 106, 107, 109, 111, 113, 121, 122, 123, 124, 125, 126, 128, 132, 133, 134, 136, 139, 140, 142, 145, 146, 147, 148, 150, 152, 153, 154, 160
Whence, 70, 91, 108
Whenever, 61, 116
Where, 62, 70, 72, 77, 89, 102, 107, 109, 112, 113, 120, 121, 122, 126, 128, 135, 139, 140, 141, 143, 150
Wherever, 98, 144
Wherry, 140
Whether, 27, 68, 88, 93, 143, 149, 155, 160
Which, 26, 33, 38, 39, 41, 45, 46, 47, 48, 54, 55, 56, 58, 60, 63, 64, 70, 72, 73, 74, 76, 77, 78, 79, 80, 83, 85, 87, 88, 90, 92, 95, 96, 101,

104, 105, 106, 107, 108, 109, 110, 113, 114, 115, 117, 119, 120, 121, 124, 125, 130, 133, 139, 140, 142, 144, 145, 146, 147, 148, 149, 152, 153, 154, 155, 156, 160
While, 25, 51, 59, 67, 70, 75, 102, 110, 111, 114, 122, 128, 132, 134, 142, 145, 147, 148, 157
Whipcord, 75
Whispered, 132
Whispering, 158
White, 73, 141, 148, 153, 159
Whitethroat, 122
Whittled, 152
Who, 26, 34, 36, 37, 40, 41, 48, 51, 59, 61, 67, 70, 75, 80, 81, 90, 91, 95, 96, 98, 100, 107, 112, 116, 118, 123, 129, 135, 137, 144, 145, 151, 152, 154, 155
Whoever, 122
Whole, 27, 41, 76, 79, 124, 126, 129
Wholly, 60, 78, 149
Whom, 43, 61, 105
Whose, 80, 91, 105, 124, 137
Whosoever, 45
Why, 92, 132, 145, 151, 157
Wicked, 105
Wide, 158
Widen, 156
Wife, 114
Wild, 72, 123, 138, 142
Wilder, 87, 92
Wilderness, 89, 107
Wildflowers, 138
Will, 22, 24, 28, 32, 34, 37, 40, 56, 57, 63, 69, 70, 81, 83, 86, 88, 90, 93, 94, 96, 98, 105, 109, 113, 115, 119, 122, 145, 147, 150, 151, 153, 155, 158
William, 70, 81, 101
Willing, 29, 60, 90, 103
Willow, 140
Willows, 142
Wilson, 128
Win, 151
Wind, 31, 52, 55, 74, 77, 138, 141, 142
Wind's, 141
Windowpanes, 129
Windows, 47, 102
Winds, 79
Wine, 29
Wing, 59
Winged, 112
Wings, 70, 102
Winston, 32
Winter, 47, 79, 92, 109, 142
Wintry, 31
Wiped, 145

Wise, 29, 70, 122
Wiser, 96
Wisest, 98
Wish, 60, 91, 144
Wished, 95
Wished-for, 151
Wishes, 85
Wishing, 66
With, 22, 23, 27, 28, 29, 34, 35, 39, 40, 42, 43, 46, 50, 51, 52, 53, 55, 57, 58, 60, 62, 63, 64, 66, 68, 69, 70, 71, 72, 73, 74, 75, 78, 79, 80, 83, 84, 85, 86, 87, 91, 92, 93, 94, 95, 97, 98, 99, 100, 101, 102, 103, 104, 105, 106, 108, 111, 112, 113, 117, 118, 119, 120, 121, 122, 124, 125, 126, 127, 128, 130, 132, 133, 134, 137, 138, 140, 141, 142, 143, 145, 146, 148, 150, 152, 153, 154, 156, 157, 160
Withdrew, 115
Wither, 112
Withered, 47
Within, 66, 91
Without, 23, 40, 59, 67, 69, 76, 90, 95, 114, 118, 132, 136
Withstand, 100
Wits, 61
Wizard, 153
Woke, 99
Wolf, 100
Woman, 141
Woman's, 100
Womankind, 90
Women, 90, 99
Won't, 147
Wonder, 125
Wondered, 74
Wonderful, 59, 68, 71, 74, 92, 146
Wonders, 120, 133, 148
Wood, 70, 97, 142
Wooden, 66, 102
Woods, 89, 92, 100, 126, 138
Wooed, 79
Word, 56, 86, 94, 136, 157
Words, 59, 94, 128, 144, 157
Wordsworth, 70, 81, 101
Wore, 33
Work, 27, 41, 62, 63, 85, 95, 97, 111, 115, 121, 126, 129, 136, 137, 145, 152, 155
Worked, 46, 84
Worker, 137
Working, 152
Workmen, 102
Works, 145
World, 25, 26, 30, 45, 52, 61, 64, 70, 82, 85, 88, 90, 92, 113, 115, 119, 124, 131, 139, 155
Worldly, 94

Worn, 123, 153
Worry, 147
Worse, 66, 78
Worship, 136
Worth, 20, 29, 63, 90
Worthy, 21, 116
Would, 30, 33, 43, 56, 63, 64, 67, 68, 69, 72, 74, 75, 81, 84, 88, 96, 97, 100, 104, 111, 115, 120, 121, 123, 124, 127, 130, 131, 135, 146, 150, 154
Wrap, 159
Wreck, 22
Wretch, 91
Wretchedly, 78
Wretches, 126
Wrinkles, 33
Write, 71, 113, 157
Writer, 51, 69
Writing, 48, 51, 152
Written, 130, 157
Wrong, 21
Wronged, 123
Wrote, 113, 132, 157
Wrought, 95, 108
Wyss, 114, 144

X, Y, Z

Yard, 83, 137, 150
Yates, 36
Ye, 105
Year, 46, 79, 87, 89, 144, 149
Year's, 87
Years, 68, 118, 125, 129, 137, 144, 149, 155
Yellow, 158
Yelping, 100
Yes, 88, 139, 157, 158
Yesterday, 58, 96
Yet, 32, 43, 49, 53, 57, 63, 73, 79, 84, 85, 86, 89, 106, 109, 110, 113, 114, 119, 120, 126, 142
Yokel, 96
Yonder, 85, 154
York, 80
You, 24, 29, 32, 46, 57, 63, 67, 69, 83, 86, 90, 92, 93, 98, 104, 106, 116, 119, 122, 123, 124, 139, 145, 146, 147, 154, 157, 158
You're, 157
Young, 29, 54, 80, 85, 95, 110, 113, 119, 130, 132, 134, 135, 137, 144, 145, 146, 154
Youngest, 113, 134
Your, 46, 63, 83, 86, 93, 98, 106, 119, 123, 137, 145, 146, 157
Yours, 83, 90
Youths, 140